The Cosmic Center

The Cosmic Center

The Supremacy of Christ in a Secular Wasteland

D. BRUCE LOCKERBIE

MULTNOMAH · PRESS

Portland, Oregon 97266

Edited by Rodney L. Morris
Cover design and illustration by Britt Taylor Collins

THE COSMIC CENTER
©1977, 1986 by Multnomah Press
Portland, Oregon 97266

Printed in the United States of America

Library of Congress Cataloging-in-Publication Data

Lockerbie, D. Bruce.
  The cosmic center.

  "Revised edition"—
  Includes indexes.
  1. Christianity and culture.   2. Secularism.   3. Jesus Christ—Person and offices.   I. Title.
BF115.C8L6   1986   261   85-18741
ISBN 0-88070-132-3

85   86   87   88   89   90   –   10   9   8   7   6   5   4   3   2   1

To Don and Ruth Fonseca,
friends and fellow-workers.

Things fall apart, the center cannot hold.
William Butler Yeats
"The Second Coming"

The nearer anything lies to that center of existence where we are concerned with the whole, that is, with man's relation to God and the being of the person, the greater the disturbance of rational knowledge by sin . . .
Emil Brunner
Revelation and Reason

At the still point of the turning world. Neither flesh nor fleshless;
Neither from nor towards; at the still point, there the dance is,
But neither arrest nor movement. And do not call it fixity,
Where past and future are gathered. Neither movement from nor towards,
Neither ascent nor decline. Except for the point, the still point,
There would be no dance, and there is only the dance.
T. S. Eliot
Four Quartets

He is before all things, and in him all things hold together.
St. Paul
Colossians 1:17

Contents

Acknowledgments

Early drafts of this book were first presented in lecture form at various schools and colleges, universities and seminaries. I am particularly grateful to the Thomas F. Staley Foundation, which underwrote several of the lectureships for which this material was originally prepared.

Parts of the book have appeared in essays and articles published in *Christianity Today*, *The Reformed Journal*, *Eternity*, and *The New York Times Book Review*.

Many of the personal experiences and observations mentioned herein came about as a result of a world tour my family and I made during a sabbatical leave granted by The Stony Brook School.

Multnomah Press, spurred on by Rod Morris, editorial manager, has agreed to issue this second edition of *The Cosmic Center*. For his support and confidence in this book's worth, as well as for his personal friendship, I am grateful.

Throughout the process of revising and reworking this edition, I have benefited from the stimulus of discussion with friends and colleagues. I am particularly indebted to the Reverend Peter Mann and John M. Kenney for their criticism and insight.

Once again, Mary Rost prepared the manuscript but this time—a decade after the first edition—on a word processor.

During these same ten years, I have learned to rely more and more on the wisdom and encouragement of my most helpful reader and critic, my wife Lory. Her love makes my writing possible.

Introduction to the Revised Edition

All my life I've suffered from motion sickness in one form or another. As a child, the prospect of the most ordinary ride in a car carried with it the likelihood of distress. If my father chose to have me accompany him, as boy soprano singing in Dad's evangelistic meetings, he would always have to plan on sufficient driving time to allow for the obligatory roadside stops en route to our destination. We tried all the known remedies and preventive measures, but nothing worked.

As a teenager, I felt like a wallflower every time my friends and I would go to an amusement park. They all would be thrilled by the roller coaster and Ferris wheel, while I spent my time throwing darts at balloons or guessing the fat lady's weight. Once—only once—a girl friend named Lory talked me into attempting to enjoy the parachute jump at Coney Island. How we ever married four years later still amazes me!

Then we became parents of two sons, Don and Kevin, and a daughter Ellyn. The responsibility of every father, of course, obligates him to take his children to the playground. There too I was something of a failure. Every object of my children's delight spelled headache and nausea to me. I could negotiate the monkey bars, crawling over their geometric configurations, but I couldn't hang by the backs of my knees, as my children did and wished me to do also. The swings presented a similar problem: I could place a child on the seat and give the swing a healthy shove, but after that, I'd have to turn away from watching. Instead, I'd try to catch the rhythm of the swing and so, without looking, propel my child without disquieting my system.

Then there was that other contraption in most playgrounds— the metal stanchion in the ground with a wooden running board that wheels around. The child stands on the platform, and the indulgent parent pushes his child into orbit. Because the mechanism is heavy, it generally requires the parent to run while pushing, like a football lineman driving against a blocking sled. During my children's playground years, I was competing in national and international track meets; I was in good shape. But I could never last more than one lap around that tiny circle before collapsing against the nearest cyclone fence. Thereafter some other parent would have to keep my children happy.

But by far the worst form of torment was the carousel, the merry-go-round. Not only was it merrily going around, but those horses—up and down, up and down! In their own perverse way, my children yearned for the carousel. It seemed as though we seldom passed any amusement park without stopping for "just one ride." I'd try to do my duty, positioning the three children close together on adjacent ponies, then stationing myself where I could watch them all go by at once, before turning away during the rest of the circuit.

One day, we were in Manhattan, and I had charge of the children for a time while Lory shopped. We went to the Children's Zoo in Central Park; nearby stands the carousel. As we left the zoo, one of the children spied the merry-go-round, and I agreed. For some reason, on that particular day, business was slow. These three children were the only customers. They rode once, then again, while I did my compensating best to fight off motion sickness from just watching them pass by.

After the second ride, I indicated that it was time to leave. But the proprietor, whose name I later learned was Sal Napolitano, said to me, "Hey, have another ride, free this time. And, mister, you ride too." Oh no, I protested, thanking him nonetheless, and I explained to him my problem. Then I added, "I don't know how you take it, round-and-round, hour after hour, day after day." He replied, "It's no problem, not where I am," and he invited me to join him at the center of the carousel—at the center, where the switches and the gears and the power may be found.

I stood with Sal Napolitano at the center, and for the first time I knew peace.

Chapter 1

Flies in the Perfume Bottle: The Maelstrom of Modern Culture

*M*y earliest awareness of the world-at-large dates from when I was a small boy in Ontario, Canada. One morning my father was listening to a BBC broadcast, and through the static of overseas transmission I heard for the first time the ravings of Adolf Hitler in one of his tirades. "Is that the devil?" I asked.

Some months later, my elementary schoolmates and I were herded together in the school auditorium to be lectured on the part we could play in winning the war. We were to "Back the Attack," buying savings stamps at twenty-five cents apiece. To motivate us, we were shown newsreel films of the Luftwaffe's bombing raids on Britain. The screams of terror from children watching the effects of war still linger in my mind.

Not long after, in August 1942, a Canadian reconnaissance force of some seven thousand men landed at Dieppe, on the Channel coast of France. Half of them were lost in that engagement, the greatest calamity suffered by Canadian troops. Many were from our part of Ontario—fathers, husbands, brothers, sons. I've never forgotten the haunted look of sorrow on the faces of women and children in our city, in my school, in my father's church.

The measure of my life is but a handbreadth to the eternities, but in that span we've learned to compress the planet on which we live. Just yesterday, half the globe was still remote from us; its accomplishments and its atrocities were at least delayed from our hearing. Today we live in a shrunken world, a universe squeezed into a ball by the marvels of technology. "East is East, and West is West," wrote Rudyard Kipling, but he wrongly concluded that "never the twain shall meet." They have met—they meet every day—in a "Voice of America" jazz broadcast heard in New Delhi; at a Ravi Shankar concert in London; through pirated lp's and stereo tapes sold in Hong Kong; before a television screen in Taipei or at a movie theater in Bangkok; or at a Transcendental meditation class in New York.

All this has come about as a result of rapid development in communications technology. But the new uni-culture extracts a heavy toll for technology's convenience and accessibility. Culture is invaded by an encroaching, penetrating, universal sameness—like the taste of French fries throughout a chain of fast-food outlets. The price we must pay is what Arnold Toynbee called "the annihilation of distance by modern Western technology." This loss of distance permits all the tensions of the world to rush immediately into our homes.

As they returned from church services on Sunday, 24 November 1963, many Americans witnessed their first authentic murder, the televised shooting of Lee Harvey Oswald by Jack Ruby in Dallas. Today no place on Earth is too remote for the all-seeing satellite eye. Whether it be the shelling of a Middle Eastern village, a marathon runner's anguish in the Olympic stadium, an IRA shoot-out in Belfast, a hijacked plane in Zurich, or an assassination attempt in Washington, D. C., we are there.

And that is precisely the point. The pace of modern living is so accelerated and we have such easy access to so much bad news, we find ourselves participating daily, as vicarious observers, in unending cycles of catastrophe, holocaust, and human folly. They would leave us suffocated by grief if we did not defend ourselves; so we adopt a veneer of cynicism to maintain our sanity. And for relaxation? We read a murder mystery while waiting for our favorite cops-and-robbers series on TV.

Yet even more troubling than the tempo of our living and its dulling of our sensibilities is this fact: All over the world, human beings are losing their cultural identities, becoming instead an almost faceless, featureless mass, molded by technology into identical shapes. Under the pressure of what we might call the *mediacracy*, persons are being taught the truncated rhetoric of slogans from television advertising, lyrics from pop tunes, dialogue from technicolor nightmares. All over the world we're being taught to dress according to fashion, to value only what is commercial and current. These trends in speech, fashion, and values are being determined for us by technocratic managers, specialists in the new science of human control.

The world we know today is very different from the colonial empires of my childhood. Even as recently as a decade ago, it may have been appropriate to speak of "Western culture" as distinct from "Eastern culture." The grand oratorio as against temple bells and sitar. *King Lear* in contrast to a retelling of tribal lore around the village fire. Detroit's assembly line versus a solitary craftsman. The nuclear reactor or the ox at a grindstone. But no longer.

In a world diminished by supersonic travel and television satellites, Hong Kong is more "Western" than Minneapolis; Kathmandu is as commercial as Disneyland. India now has both the ox and the A-bomb. And the so-called Third World is no longer emerging but merging into a conglomerate world culture, a vast enveloping macro-culture—a veritable smorgasbord spread with Japanese sukiyaki, Manchurian hot pot, Ethiopian injera wat, Hungarian goulash, and American hot dogs. Nairobi, with its Kentucky Fried Chicken on Kenyatta Boulevard, could be Pasadena. At the night market on the streets of Taichung, Taiwan, merchants of Western-styled clothing attract the largest crowds. A bazaar in Rangamati, Bangladesh, features Bata shoes; in Kodaikanal, South India, Timex watches; and the great festering open market in Addis Ababa, European pornography. In Madras, the most popular film attraction features a black American football-star-turned-actor, Jim Brown, while Malaysian television offers American westerns and detective thrillers.

But the cultural merger is not exclusively one-way. Even while Asian teenagers ape their English-speaking counterparts in exclaiming to every pleasure, "Freaky, man!" so from Santa Barbara to Southampton Row, Anglo-Saxon youths, scalp-shaven and saffron-robed, chant their Hare Krishna litanies. An advertisement in *The New York Times*, jargon-filled with cross-cultural blending, announces a symposium on "biofeedback, Meditation, and Self-Regulatory Therapies." What the contemplative East has known for centuries as the ascent of the *kundalini*—an awakening of spiritual powers within oneself—the technological West now acclaims in cybernetic cliches at expensive weekend seminars attended by seekers after "Self-Actualization" or other narcissistic states of mind.

In almost any metropolis of the costume of today's young people testifies to a new internationalism, a leveling of culture manifest in the uniformity of their dress: West German running shoes, American blue-jeans, a West African dashiki, bracelets and beads from Afghanistan, and always a Japanese camera or Sony Walkman radio.

A fitting microcosm for today's new mega-culture is the departure lounge of any international airport. It's the model for Marshall McLuhan's "global village." In this sterile, often garish playground, the sojourner finds his literal utopia, a never-never land of tax-free trinkets beyond the scrutiny of custom officials. But suspended in limbo between here and there, the traveler slumps in his seat, his mind and body victimized by jet lag, stupefied by dysrhythmia, exhausted by lethargy, a blank expression in his eyes—a cipher indistinguishable from others around him. In his hand, his only contact with "the real thing," a bottle of Coca-Cola.

This blurring of national, religious, and often racial identities finds common ground in the dissolution, first, of concern for cultural distinctives. In the name of progress, old customs, old values, give way to a vast, neutralizing effect of sameness. "Man is to be smoothed out," warns Jacques Ellul, "like a pair of pants under a steam iron." Primary concerns, such as the search for inner contentment through spiritual sacrifice or satisfaction through submission to the authority of one's elders— these erode in derision.

I think of a typical Japanese home in the modern suburbs of Tokyo. Though it appears to retain much of its national character—the woven matting on the floor, sliding panels, a charcoal pit to warm the central room—this house also speaks of the engulfing macro-culture. In the room customarily set aside for the preservation of ancestor worship, there is still a shelf, high up on the wall, for the household gods. But underneath a new idol dominates—a 25-inch color TV set.

THE PRESERVATION OF CULTURE

Can it be that my generation, for all our faults, is the last to concern itself with the preservation of the past? The study of history, the maintenance of simple family customs, a sustaining reverence for inexplicable social taboos were all part of our upbringing. Until yesterday, *culture* was thought to be a necessary safekeeping of those elements that give meaning to our lives. For many years archaeologists and anthropologists have been studying their findings from ancient societies, both primitive and advanced. The often orderly arrangement of weapons, implements, works of art or documents, in tombs or in places of worship, seems to have served two purposes: to impress posterity as well as to appease any gods beyond the grave.

So too with modern generations until now. We have shown our yearning to be remembered and have contrived means of leaving caches of mementos behind us. The Stage Manager in Thornton Wilder's 1938 play, *Our Town*, acting as the play's narrator, tells the audience what is to be placed in the cornerstone of a new bank building in Grover's Corners, New Hampshire. He chooses representative museum pieces "for people to dig up . . . a thousand years from now"—a Bible, the Constitution, a volume of Shakespeare's works, and copies of both *The New York Times* and the village's weekly *Sentinel*.

But then the Stage Manager salvages Grover's Corners from obscurity and elevates it to stand as a microcosm for all time. He remembers that Babylon left nothing more than "the names of the kings and some copies of wheat contracts." Greece and Rome, however, provided information about "the real life of the people" through plays and poems. And so, the Stage Manager decides to include in the cornerstone a tableau of *real* life in the New Hampshire village—the script of the play in which he and his fellow townsfolk are characters:

> So I'm going to have a copy of this play put in the cornerstone and the people a thousand years from now'll know a few simple facts about us—more than the Treaty of Versailles and the Lindbergh flight.
>
> See what I mean?
>
> So—people a thousand years from now—this is the way we were in the provinces north of New York at the beginning of the twentieth century.—This is the way we were: in our growing up and in our marrying and in our living and in our dying.

If the daily drama of life becomes our metaphor, then culture is both the theater and the play—a vast, fluid, ever changing kaleidoscope of action and reaction, accretion and abatement, experiment and discard, improvised or permanently recorded. On occasion, we see ourselves as actors or audience. For some of us, our scene may conclude before the final curtain; we risk being forgotten when the time comes for applause.

So then, to preserve the fact that we performed our roles, we hope to have our names set down. Not perhaps with the *dramatis personae*, history's most important actors, but at least among those who built the set, designed the costumes, wired the lighting, played in the orchestra, or—as important as all—picked up cigar butts after each intermission. For the traditional view of culture has long believed that culture is also the maintenance of beauty, respect for order, and all else that brings sanctity to life. Culture has represented an attitude of reverence, a desire to sanctify emblems of our own worthiness—in William Butler Yeats's great phrases, "Monuments of unaging intellect . . . Monuments of its own magnificence."

To be sure, such monuments are sometimes curiously preserved. The Louvre, the Heritage, the Prado, the British Museum, the Metropolitan, yes. But in a reclaimed swamp, within sight of Manhattan's towers, lies buried a sampling of artifacts from twentieth-century Western culture.

At the 1939 World's Fair, an eight-foot metal alloy casing was solemnly lowered fifty feet into the ground, then covered with an engraved marker. Inside the tube, named by the Westinghouse Corporation "the Time Capsule," were thirty-five objects familiar to most people in Western civilization—an alarm clock, a fountain pen, a camera, a can opener, a razor, and so on. Books and periodicals on microfilm were also included. Westinghouse and the World's Fair buried the Time Capsule in an expressed hope that it would preserve some record of our culture, as it was in 1939, for peoples living some five thousand years later. A book containing the exact location of the site, calculated by longitude and latitude to within an inch of the spot, also listed and described each item in the Capsule. This record was then circulated among some three thousand museums, libraries, and other places of presumed interest throughout the world.

In 1965, at the second New York World's Fair, Westinghouse again deposited a Time Capsule, on this occasion attracting far less publicity. The new container updated its predecessor with information about atomic energy, World War II, the Dead Sea scrolls, and Roger Bannister's four-minute mile. These are among the surprises awaiting whoever finds them in the year 6939 A.D.

But the generation come to maturity since 1965 rejects the idea of culture in a capsule. Technology's "annihilation of distance" appears to invalidate traditional views of culture. The treasure trove definition is held to be a product of snobbish and elitist teaching, the remnant of a parochial mind. In many respects the new generation is right in its opinion. By treating culture like a time capsule, traditionalists have reduced it to a collection of frozen specimens from a lost age. We've been aware of a certain tone of reverence towards culture, of certain buildings where "cultural events" occur—archives, concert halls, theaters, opera houses, sometimes even churches. We're somehow convinced that culture is a good thing, that it should serve as the repository for each succeeding generation's accomplishments. But once safely stowed, the culture of our age has become a curio for the next.

The world today perceives that such a notion of culture has helped older generations to perpetuate the status quo. "This is the way your forefathers lived; this too is the way you will live." No, says the new cosmopolite, the citizen of a unified world culture. Culture is an organic, continuously growing event. Culture is now! And so the generations struggle over the opinion that culture must now mean the death of the past.

Into this controversy comes another voice seeking to balance traditional with revolutionary attitudes towards culture. This advocate holds that, while culture is today's shared experience, culture must also preserve from the past those achievements most worthy of memory. Culture doesn't only hang on gallery walls, it walks the streets beside us, holding us responsible to assess its value by standards whose worth has also been tested. Culture is the product of human endeavor to burn away the dross and leave only the most enduring testament to human imagination. Culture defines humanity's confrontation here and now with the mystery of transcendence, the certain knowledge of something else beyond oneself. Culture is man's contribution to God's ongoing creation.

According to this view of culture, the God who created man to image forth his Creator also commissioned him to reproduce beauty wherever he could fashion it, to celebrate love in song, to adorn nature with evidences of his joy in living, to nurture and tend the Garden of God, to delight in the fact of existence, to pleasure himself with the play of his fancy. All this was to be done in fulfillment of the mandate given in Genesis 1:28, "'Be fruitful and increase in number; fill the earth and subdue it. Rule over the fish of the sea and the birds of the air and over every living creature that moves on the ground.'" And so, at Flushing Meadow and at Grover's Corners, in the Lascaux caves and on Easter Island, the human race continues to assert itself against the erasures of time.

This was first the Hebrew, then the Christian, view of human responsibility to God and to one's neighbor. From this sense of individual responsibility grew, in time, an enormous power constituted in an Established Church and its political authority. From such authority, spanning at one time all of Europe and reaching into North Africa and even to parts of the Far East, as well as westward to the New World, quite naturally flowed the art and music, literature and vernacular that became Western civilization. Indeed, the foundations of European and North American culture are deeply ingrained with the mark of Christian religiosity. Medieval Europe and later her colonies became known as "Christendom," meaning that from the rise of Constantine in the fourth century A.D. until the assault of rationalism in the seventeenth century, the governing influence of Christian presuppositions held sway throughout the Western world.

These presuppositions maintained that God—the Triune Father, Son, and Spirit—created, redeemed, and sustained the universe; that his nature is beneficent and just, but that disobedience is sin and must be atoned for. According to Christian doctrine, this atonement could not be achieved by man himself; rather, the inspired Scriptures taught "that God was reconciling the world to himself in Christ, not counting men's sins against them" (2 Corinthians 5:19).

This act of reconciliation had been accomplished at a specific point in history, when God chose to manifest himself as a human being—a Jew, Jesus of Nazareth, during the reign of the Roman emperors Augustus and Tiberius, in the tiny provinces of Galilee and Judea. That Jesus was the divinely appointed Messenger or Messiah was confirmed in his glorious resurrection from the dead. Further confirmation will come with his expected and imminent return from heaven, an apocalyptic event that will also bring about the consummation of human history and the restoration of the Kingdom of God. Until that time, those who believe constitute a witnessing body known as the church, beloved of God and responsible for the care of his creation.

In these creedal terms, Christians might see culture as evidence of finite human aspiration toward the infinite. However bent, distorted, or even perverse human culture may become, it nonetheless remains an expression by man—God's own imitator—and therefore precious to God.

THE DEBASEMENT OF CULTURE

Yet today, the world no longer accepts these Christian presuppositions. "Western civilization," wrote Toynbee, "that is now unifying the world in these various ways is a post-Christian or ex-Christian civilization." With the retreat of Christianity, its cultural mandate also declines into chaos. Another view of culture has taken its place, an attitude derived from the secular vision of human existence. Without absolutes, without aesthetic principles, without criteria for taste, without moral direction, contemporary culture careens in trackless shambles. The dance has been abandoned, the riot has begun, with little or no concern for its consequences, as the Stage Manager says, "in our living and in our dying."

Something foul now contaminates the sweet aroma of life, like flies in the perfume bottle. Something cheap reduces every human aspiration to its lowest common denominator of greed and lust. To us whose heritage has been traditional Western culture, buttressed by the Christian vision of life, the crisis seems particularly acute. Again, the village in *Our Town* serves as a model: To a question regarding "culture or love of beauty in Grover's Corners," the newspaper editor replies:

> Well, ma'am, there ain't much—not in the sense you mean. . . . *Robinson Crusoe* and the Bible; and Handel's "Largo," we all know that; and Whistler's "Mother"—those are just about as far as we go.

Today one wonders if the average English-speaking town can make even so modest a claim. In North America, at least, we've become a continent of philistines, engorged by trivia, yet as culturally malnourished as children fed only on lollipops. For music, we have MTV's rock videos; for art, graffiti and painting by numbers; for sculpture, dashboard icons and lawn statues; for literature, the Harlequin novels; for drama, soap operas and game shows. Our means of discourse has been minimized to depend largely upon grunts and that all-purpose substitute for thought, "Y' know." Our tastes are determined by pollsters and ratings. This week's Top Forty recordings are next week's Golden Oldies. Whereas ancient Greece knew the difference in aesthetics and moral tone between tragedy and comedy, we seem to have lost that power to discriminate. The result, in our theaters and in our public life, is a juxtaposition of the ridiculous with the contemptible, the outrageous with the unspeakable.

"We are a Grade B mediocre people culturally," says one commentator, and no wonder. The academy, once an interpreter of culture to the inquiring mind, has abdicated its intellectual authority. The pose adopted reinforces a professional strategy aimed at offering students what they want rather than what they need to learn; many teachers today no longer claim to know what succeeding generations ought to remember from the past. Increasingly, therefore, such teachers perpetuate cycles of ignorance in which they themselves have been caught. For the past thirty years, test scores for graduate school candidates have been reflecting a disastrous trend: the lowest scores are registered by aspiring primary and secondary school teachers. Overall, American education simply is not receiving the benefit of the nation's best minds.

Should we, then, be shocked to hear that "a rising tide of mediocrity" threatens to engulf our schools? Not if we accept the premise put forward by the Reverend Raymond A. Schroth, Dean of the College of the Holy Cross, that much of today's debacle in education stems from "a silent conspiracy among students, teachers, and parents in which no one will bother anyone else."

> Parents set social and economic, rather than intellectual, goals for the young; then they pursue their own social lives. Teachers give little or no homework, and so, with no papers to mark one can spend the week watching a TV miniseries. Rather than read, high school students hang out, watch soaps and sitcoms, and play video games. They do not complain about not being challenged, so long as they get good grades and get into college. Then it is too late.

Even among the best educated in our society, respect for quality and lasting worth rarely rises above the level of self-mockery. We display as coffee table ornaments huge books reproducing paintings from famous galleries never visited. And do we read the books? We play piecemeal recordings, snippets of love themes from Tchaikovsky. We call it *culture*, but it is at best an ersatz culture served up to us in sterile, prepackaged doses, like freeze-dried foods and just as tasteless. We call it *art*, but it is art prostituted until it becomes merely the familiar arranged for our easy assimilation.

Why has modern culture changed so radically? Perhaps one answer lies in the fact that the Christian view of individual worth has been lost. For when that sense of worth is abandoned, there is no longer any need to conserve anything. The Christian view of man's worth gave him something to live for now and in the future. The resurrection promise, that because Jesus lives we too shall live, confirms Christian presuppositions concerning the sanctity of each person's life, guaranteeing immortality, its opposite feeds upon the finality of death. Here, then, is a primary difference between Christianity and secularism, for what is secularism if not a view of the world and man's place in it that centers upon temporal and material concerns? Paul spelled it out for the Corinthians: "So we fix our eyes not on what is seen, but on what is unseen. For what is seen is temporary, but what is unseen is eternal" (2 Corinthians 4:18).

But in our age, the presuppositions of supernatural Christian belief are held to be quaint at best; the presuppositions governing our culture are wholly secular. In America, for example, we are what the social historian Max Lerner calls "a people absorbed with energy and speed, communication and power." Secularism appeals to this temporal fascination, disallowing any possible reality to be found in eternal or spiritual concerns. Secularism finds no place for powers greater than man himself, unless they are the untamed and untamable powers of nature— like man, also random and chaotic, accidental and uncaused. Discovering that he is present in the universe only by chance, Secular Man takes luck to be his highest good and lives by the gambler's creed in a cosmic casino.

For secularism, there is of course no God, no transcendent nor immanent creative, redeeming force; nor is there need for any. Secularism, as Karl Heim once wrote, is "the state of mind in which the question of God and his existence is no longer a question at all." Not that secularism is irreligious or atheistic. On the contrary, secularism is fanatically committed to principles which it holds religiously and to gods worshiped devoutly. Secular man has his own gospel, the gospel of Making It. His scriptures are *The Wall Street Journal*, *The Financial Times*, *Playboy* and *Penthouse*, the Neiman-Marcus or Harrod's department store catalogue. His hymnal includes "The Impossible Dream" and "I Did It My Way."

Still, even for the secularist, death looms, and in the face of its inevitability secularism adopts defenses, stratagems, and brave postures to confront this reality. A long-running television commercial for beer illustrates one of secularism's accommodations. The viewer sees a group of sailors racing to the top of the mast on a full-rigged schooner; or a contingent of merchant marines newly arrived in some exotic port—always folk heroes from our fantasies whose advice is, "You only go around once in life, so grab for all the gusto you can."

Clearly, the advertising writers have aimed their pitch at something to gratify us *now*, as if now were all we should ever know. The highest aim of secularism is satisfaction at the moment. But because that moment is mercurial, always slipping out of our grasp, satisfaction—even if obtained—never lasts. So secularism insists that we repeat the moment, repeat whatever experience it is that gratifies us—recapture the thrill, the titillation, the high. And what we do, we must do now and with gusto! Because we get only one chance.

So, without daring explicitly to remind its audience of potential customers that death is a fact, the beer commercial nonetheless points at mutability and decay, at death's ineluctable reality. "One day," the commercial says in effect, "all this vitality, all this youthfulness and strength, all this physical beauty will be gone. All you'll have left will be the memories or regrets. You only go around once in life, so go for the gusto, or don't go at all."

An advertisement in Carnegie Hall's concert program sells luxury apartments with the same kind of sales pitch:

> Nobody gets out of life alive. So it makes superb
> common sense to live as beautifully, as comfortably
> and as creatively as possible while one has the time.
> Life is too short to settle for second best.

Secularism's search for the gusto of life is also a struggle against the swift passage of time, life's inevitable mutability and decay. "Carpe diem!" Seize the day, Secular Man exhorts himself, because, as Andrew Marvell's impatient lover tells his coy mistress,

> at my back I always hear
> Time's winged chariot hurrying near.

No wonder so many men and women wander through their nights and days like animated dolls in Toyland, chasing each other around the Prickly Pear, caught up in the frenzy of each day's new diversion. Drained of spiritual values and the promise of eternal life, reduced to the subexistence of a robot, the children of secularism have been perfectly described by T. S. Eliot in "The Hollow Men":

> Shape without form, shade without color,
> Paralysed force, gesture without motion.

But even if the wind-up toy should run down, Secular Man isn't left without his resources. His immediate goal, according to Iranian philosopher F. M. Esfandiary, is "to overcome aging and, in time, death itself." To Esfandiary, "it is outrageous that such a beautiful phenomenon as intelligent, sentient life should be encased in such fleeting vulnerable bodies." The solution, as he sees it, lies in a gradual replacement of diseased organs with biotechnical substitutes. Malcolm Muggeridge views this prospect with horror, wryly calling it "transplant surgery with a view to changing our spare parts as they wear out and so keeping us on the road indefinitely like vintage cars."

But to Esfandiary and others, overcoming physical death is too serious a matter for joking. "We will continue to de-animalize our bodies," he claims, "creating new durable attractive physiologies." If these should fail, there is yet another recourse: anabiosis or return to life through cyrogenics, which means "freezing the body immediately after death until a suitable time in the future when the body can be revived" through injections of newly developed restorative drugs.

As medical technology becomes more sophisticated and life-sustaining systems more advanced, secularism narrows its own minimal definition of what it means to be a human being. At no point does the scientism of secularity concede any possibility that human beings might possess spirit as well as flesh. It never occurs to secularism that the mind might be something greater than a metaphor to describe cortical impulses or programmed responses to biochemical stimuli. Spiritual dimension is a curiosity foreign to Secular Man, preoccupied as he is with contemporaneity and material progress through the wonder-workings of technology.

In a landmark case, the parents of Karen Ann Quinlan, described by doctors as being kept alive mechanically though in "a persistent vegetative state," petitioned the courts to have the machines at their daughter's bedside turned off. "I don't want her to die," said her father, "I just want to put her back in her natural state and leave her to the Lord. If the Lord wants her to live, she'll live. If he wants her to die, she'll die." And later, Joseph Quinlan spoke of the tragedy of preventing his daughter from passing out of this sphere and into the glory of eternal life in the presence of God. Politeness and compassion for the Quinlan family blunted any public mockery of their faith in life-after-death.

But secularism cannot be counted on to treat such expressions dispassionately. There is too much at stake. The problem has already gone beyond questions of euthanasia or "death with dignity"; the problem now is to decide at what point to assert the priority of mechanical life-support over the natural. Because secularism rejects any beliefs in an after-life, it must delay the last mortal breath for as long as possible, even after the brain has lost all power to reason, the body all control of its functions. There will still be the instruments of technology, for as Toynbee pointed out, "the surviving features of the Christian way of life are now . . . no longer our civilization's distinctive features." Instead, "the distinctive feature of our Western civilization is obviously its technology."

Of course, technology in itself is morally neutral, without responsibility, as is a typewriter without responsibility for the libel its mechanism may produce, or an automobile without responsibility for the vehicular homicide its driver commits. But technology has been elevated by Secular Man to a position of inordinate esteem precisely because of what it represents—the means to justify Eden's primary lie, "Of course you will not die!" and its corollary, "You will be like gods."

To be like gods means to be deathless, immortal, invincible, invulnerable to the lesser forces of the cosmos, self-energized, needing nothing, wholly free. "Cursed be that mortal interindebtedness which will not do away with ledgers," cries

Captain Ahab in *Moby-Dick*. "I would be free as air: and I'm down in the whole world's books." Secular Man will not concede so readily. He is certain that he can be free, although he has chosen to reject any divine offer of freedom. He will instead free himself, if only he can obtain the power to govern himself and his environment, without responsibility to anyone or anything, and so liberate himself from fear of death. Ironically, while denying Christian immortality, Secular Man seeks to win his own. The genius behind technology now deceives him into believing that he has almost accomplished that end.

The Swiss theologian Emil Brunner describes Secular Man's technology as

> the product of the man who wants to redeem himself by rising above nature, who wants to gather life into his hand, who wants to owe his existence to nobody but himself, who wants to create a world after his own image, an artificial world which is entirely his creation. Behind the terrifying, crazy tempo of technical evolution, there is all the insatiability of secularized man who, not believing in God or eternal life, wants to snatch as much of this world within his lifetime as he can.

Brunner then sums up his analysis:

> Modern technics is, to put it crudely, the expression of the world-voracity of modern man, and the tempo of its development is the expression of his inward unrest, the disquiet of the man who is destined for God's eternity but has himself rejected this destiny.

In this post-Christian world, to use Toynbee's phrase—a world where the Lordship of Jesus Christ isn't acknowledged—Secular Man's voracious obsession with temporal power stamps its imprint upon his culture. It stands, as the aged apostle John wrote, for "everything in the world—the cravings of sinful man, the lust of his eyes and the boasting of what he has and does" (1 John 2:16). But before such an obsession can overrun the human race, the sanctity of the individual self must be sacrificed to the will of the all-engulfing macro-culture. To accomplish this end, secularism must first sweep away all thought of supernatural theism; for doesn't the existence of a personal God—Creator and Redeemer—demand the corollary fact that his creatures are of some worth? Thus the need to eliminate such a God from personal and national consciousness. Thereafter follows the dehumanizing process, transforming the human individual into an anonymous biped without feathers, faceless, nameless, stripped of individual powers of choice, dependent upon the herd impulse, enslaved by group-think, enthralled by the propaganda of the Party and the State.

With the loss of individual identity also vanish the stabilizing effects of reverence and awe for the dignity of the human body, for the life of the mind, for things of the spirit. Into the vacuum thus created rush the vagaries of secular values to engorge modern civilization in its maelstrom.

Chapter 2

Cracked Cisterns: The Symptoms of Secularism

We live in the most prosperous era in history. We're the most well-fed, widely traveled, literate people of any age. Ironically, we also live in one of the most impoverished periods in history. Even in the affluent, industrialized Western hemisphere millions are malnourished. In spite of jet travel and global television, we remain provincial. We can scarcely claim that compulsory education has resulted in a wise and just society.

If Charles Dickens were writing our tale, perhaps he would also call our epoch "the best of times, . . . the worst of times."

We pride ourselves on our advanced civilization, the keystone of which is our technological progress. We laud our accomplishments—men on the moon, libraries on microfiche, mind-expanding drugs, instant replay, data banks, organ transplants—everything except a cure for cancer and the common cold. We have somewhat less to say about the paradox that marks and mars human experience—wretchedness in the midst of wealth, discontent in the face of abundance, neuroses at the gateway of Nirvana, the symptoms of secularism.

33

MATERIALISM

The signature of our civilization is our attitude toward material things. This exaltation of mere object over and beyond the importance of spirit, and of persons as spiritual beings, helps to define secularism. North America, Western Europe, Japan, parts of Africa, Asia, and Latin America are reaping what we have so carefully sowed in the generation since the end of World War II—a harvest of the fruits of secularism, cultivated by appeals to our egos, to our natural indolence, to our common fears, to our longstanding curiosity over gimmick and gimcrackery. We need no welter of words to explain what is happening to us and through us and around us. Ralph Waldo Emerson said it plainly enough in two lines:

Things are in the saddle,
And ride mankind.

An understanding of things and the hold they have upon industrialized societies seems fundamental to a grasp of secular materialism. Once we come to comprehend, if only faintly, the stranglehold of things upon modern men and women, we may come to understand much more fully what Emerson meant when he also wrote, "Things are of the snake."
Another poet put it this way:

The world is too much with us; late and soon,
Getting and spending, we lay waste our powers.

William Wordsworth was right: "Getting and spending," the lust to acquire, the lust to consume, are the hallmarks of Secular Man. Of the secular materialist, as well as of the cynic, Oscar Wilde might have said that he is "a man who knows the price of everything and the value of nothing." W. A. Swanberg describes the multi-millionaire William Randolph Hearst as a man "gripped by an uncontrollable urge to buy, buy, buy. . . . His utter lack of self-discipline was never more evident than in the helpless, compulsive way he spent, spent, spent."
Secular Man is both wholly acquisitive and wholly waste-

ful, relying on things to bring him status and comfort. As an example, the automobile comes to mind. In most countries, to own even one motor car for some period of one's life is a luxury, an inestimable mark of success. Even in the supposedly non-materialistic countries of Asia and Africa, the automobile serves as a symbol of prestige. At the airport in Madras, an enterprising taxi driver, with perhaps the oldest American-made Hudson automobile still operating, points sneeringly at his competitors' Indian-made Ambassadors and says, "Should the American ride in such little cars? Why, no!" Of course, one pays twice as much for the privilege of riding in the Hudson.

At an embassy reception in Addis Ababa, one sees that even the poorest nations, to avoid giving the impression of backwardness, must transport their diplomats in Mercedes-Benz limousines costing fifty thousand dollars and more in Ethiopia. The paradox of representatives from starving Sahel countries being chauffeured in luxurious automobiles demonstrates the power of secular materialism—"the lust of the flesh, the lust of the eye, the pride of life." Gone are those virtues usually thought to be concomitant with spirituality—austerity, temperance, self-denial. And one can scarcely avoid wondering how many of those same spokesmen for Third World governments would rise the next day in Africa Hall to excoriate the United States of America and other perpetrators of materialistic oppression.

Meanwhile in America, in spite of energy crises and spiraling cost, the two-car and three-car family continues its buying and selling, much to Detroit's delight. Only one problem confronts us: What to do with unwanted used cars? New restrictions on junk car lots and laws against abandoning cars on streets and highways stand in our way.

Across Long Island from my home in Stony Brook, the men who operate the Islip Speedway have a solution. Every year they host the national Demolition Derby, an orgy of wreck and ruination perfectly fitting Thorstein Veblen's "theory of conspicuous consumption." In England, where the same event is held at Harringay, it's called the "Death Destruction Derby."

In both cases, the object is the same—to eliminate every competitor by smashing your auto into his so that it breaks down. The usual technique is to ram every other car in reverse, thereby protecting your own car's radiator and other essential parts.

Just to complicate matters, the Islip track is a figure-eight, heightening the likelihood of collisions as cars reach the crossover point. Occasional impediments such as a huge concrete ball add to the terror of the drivers and the ecstasy of their screaming fans. As another means of stimulating interest, promoters of these follies have recently up-graded the class of automobiles competing. No more Fords. Now it's Cadillacs and Continentals at Islip, Jaguars and Rolls Royces at Harringay.

The point is that spectators love the mayhem, and the more costly the object being destroyed, the more pleasure they find in its destruction. An official at Islip has said, "Our customers don't care who wins. They come to see the wrecks." One wonders, incidentally, if the same may not be true of the hundreds of thousand who flock to automobile races such as the Indianapolis 500, where not long ago three men were killed as a result of accidents in the same race.

Some psychologists propose a theory that the automobile may be the American male's substitute for a fantasized sexual playmate. If there is any validity to this speculation, the implications of a demolition derby and its corollary to staggering divorce statistics are reason enough to tremble.

"We develop a throw-away mentality to match our throw-away products," says Alvin Toffler in *Future Shock*. Such a mentality reveals itself when plenty leads to boredom and to easy discard, whether of things or of persons.

Other so-called sporting events also represent secular materialism and its contempt for the body as an emblem of a higher reality. Our bestial sports aren't auto racing or even ice hockey, brutal as these may be. They're at least conducted under rules governing fair play. In fact, recently a grand jury set a precedent for professional sport, indicting a National Hockey League player for aggravated assault, the result of a brawl during a hockey game. But at the level of sheer barbarous arena entertainment, these sports are tame.

The most offensive are "roller games"—a melee on roller skates—and what passes for wrestling among professional strongmen. Devoid of rules, these mockeries of true sport, with their obligatory interludes of outrage and maiming, pander to audiences of screaming, sweaty, lank-haired women and their doltish husbands. In them the glamorization of cruelty, the obscenity of dirty play, and the ethics of the bear-pit and the brothel fuse to form a paradigm of secular morality. The Romans and Carthaginians behaved much the same way, of course, but they were at least honest enough to admit that the name of the game played out in their circuses was really "The Cheapness of Human Life."

So too with sex. The ultimate acquisition for the secularist is the being of someone else. Dante chose to portray Satan, in the Ninth Circle of the Inferno, eternally devouring his victims. In much the same way, Secular Man seeks to devour both those who love and those who threaten him. The easiest access to *being* is *body* because, says Malcolm Muggeridge, "sex is the only mysticism offered by materialism, whose other toys—like motor-cars and aeroplanes and moving pictures and swimming-pools and flights to the moon—soon pall."

Thus sexual conquest becomes even more important than the ownership and control of blocks of shares on Wall Street. For with each conquest comes a sense of power, the assurance that through what is legally and accurately called "carnal knowledge," one has achieved total domination of another human being. But just as the plethora of automobiles brings on its own malaise, so promiscuous sex soon reduces itself to little more than the handling of raw meat—a butcher shop ordeal in which human flesh is measured and graded by the inch or by the pound.

Have you also noticed the trend in television commercials toward apocalyptic visions and extra-dimensional saviors? Following the breakthrough of the film *Close Encounters of the Third Kind*, advertising agencies now market the most mundane products in supra-terrestrial packaging. A soft glow on the horizon beckons the gaze of ordinary citizens upward and beyond. Suddenly the glow increases to a dazzling incandescence as these earthbound observers stare in wonder. And what is the subject of their visionary fascination? What deliverance is at hand? A better tasting margarine, perhaps, or an all-day deodorant, a more rambunctious pick-up truck or a pair of designer jeans. Yet no sense of silliness, no aftertaste of anticlimax, pervades these multi-million dollar productions. For while the secular mind contradicts both the spiritual and the supernatural, it borrows from the innermost convictions of the human soul in order to assert the transcendence of the trivial. By spoofing its own values, secular materialism diminishes its fears and eliminates any need to puzzle out the future.

The slogan for secular materialism has always been, "There's plenty more where that came from!" The doctrine of use and abuse is exemplified in deliberate destruction or in casual discard of an object once cherished. To encourage himself in his licentiousness, Secular Man has chosen to identify with the energy and power inherent in machines he supposes will enable him at last to control his own destiny.

But now, as the twentieth century closes upon us, we have suddenly discovered that the bounty has come to an end; the wells have gone dry. Furthermore, those machines by which Secular Man had expected to gain mastery over his environment no longer seem to recognize the master. A. M. Rosenthal of *The New York Times* offers this pessimistic observation:

> Human societies have been through all sorts of crises—wars, rebellions, plagues. Now it seems to me that we are approaching a new kind of crisis— The Age of Mechanical Disobedience.

As the reality of "mechanical disobedience"—a science fiction horror show—bursts in upon us, men everywhere seem to be in the clutches of The Great Fear.

No one can be precise about naming a date on which The Great Fear became known, but perhaps Tuesday, 9 November

1965, will do as well as any. On that date, the Western world experienced the first random failure of its life-sustaining technology, and thirty million persons in the Northeastern United States and Canada lost their sight, their cooking and heating, their transportation, their means of amusement—inexplicably and without warning. It was the first hint of Western society's vulnerability.

Industrialized into inertia, computerized into complacency, the megalopolis trapezoid covering New York to Buffalo and Toronto to Montreal suddenly discovered itself languishing in the night, without benefit of man-made power to generate electricity. A relay located near Niagara Falls, Ontario, had failed, sending back upon the Northeast cooperative power grid a surge of electric power greater than its generators could sustain. And so, across Ontario and Quebec, New York, Connecticut, Massachusetts, Vermont, and parts of Pennsylvania, New Jersey, and New Hampshire, the lights went out.

From all accounts, there was no real panic, very little looting of stores helpless without electric burglar alarms, almost no loss of life. Yet in the aftermath, in spite of experts' explanations, The Great Fear began to show itself—a nameless, numbing fear that the dimming of a few thousand light bulbs might somehow herald the coming of an eventual technological holocaust, casting civilization eternally into outer darkness.

Although the holocaust has not occurred, we have not overcome that fear. With the passing of time has come an increase in technological disasters—spillage from supertankers, the Union Carbide catastrophe in Bophal, India, threats of meltdown from nuclear plants such as Three Mile Island, an unthinkable lapse by the master computer that sends a random missile screaming toward an unintended target. Such industrial and military accidents, combined with our growing realization of the exhaustibility of Earth's resources, make us even more afraid.

Somewhere within every sensible person lodges the knowledge that, unless Western society in particular and the whole global technological complex in general change our

manner of living, we are capable of allowing either of two in-
evitabilities to overtake us. Either we'll use up all the natural
resources of food and energy production available, or else, in
our foolish reliance upon alleged "fail-safe" systems, we'll be
destroyed while we daydream.

Throughout the West, something very telling is happening. We are losing our grip, our sense of well-being, nationally
as well as personally. Nowhere is this instability more apparent
than among delegates at the United Nations who represent the
former "Western powers." Their authority, in spite of whatever
veto power they retain, has been wrested from them; it now resides, as we all know, in the pocketbooks and bank accounts of
sheikhs and mullahs whose control of oil strangles Europe,
North America, Japan, and any other nation not belonging to
the oil-producing bloc. Some political seers expect no other
solution than armed confrontation between oil producers and oil
consumers to settle the question of territorial rights versus
planetary rights to global resources. If such a confrontation
should come, it could well be the Armageddon of prophecy.

Meanwhile, loyalties on every hand are crumbling. Loyalty to the nation and its symbols of pride has been shattered in
state after state by scandal and betrayal. Loyalty to institutions,
loyalty to family—swept away in a flood of cynicism. Age-old
religious maxims have been revised so that today we no longer
inquire "Am I my brother's keeper?" and "Who is my neighbor?" except as questions of self-preservation. We feel the need
to know our brother's condition and our neighbor's where-
abouts to keep them honest, to let them know they can't get
away with anything.

In America, locksmiths are capitalizing on an ever-
growing crime rate. Daily radio and television advertisements
promise to install burglar-proof locks and quadruple locks
strong enough to withstand the force of a high-powered rifle.
New apartment buildings stress their sophisticated networks of
closed circuit cameras to monitor all comings-and-goings; they
also boast of their "uniformed receptionists," a euphemism for
armed guards.

People are scared! We are frightened by the threat of violence committed against us in our homes, to say nothing of our fear of unsafe streets and parks. More and more, city dwellers are becoming prisoners in their own custody, afraid to venture out after dark, afraid to open a window, playing the psychologically dangerous game of "Kitty-bar-the-door" with all its paranoid consequences.

Neither man's inventiveness nor his material provision has been able to secure the future against the dangers of the unknown. So Secular Man races from refuge to refuge, hoping, like Ernest Hemingway's Nick Adams—himself shell-shocked and wounded—to find a haven, a retreat from anxiety.

Hemingway's hero headed for Michigan's north woods. A half-century later, we need not go so far, for to help us escape life in the city, here comes an entrepreneur ready to profit from our fears. He owns a tract of land somewhere on the fringes of the megalopolis. First, he invents a cute name—try "Birnam Wood," "Egdon Heath," or "Vanity Fair." Then he throws together a plywood-and-plastic bungalow, sprinkles a little rye seed, and plants a soup can with a flag growing out of it. A publicist and a trick photographer produce a brochure, and the next thing we know, we're being told about a divine new retirement community for adults forty-eight years and over, complete with a championship golf course.

Then comes the pitch, thrown perhaps by someone we trust, an Art Linkletter or Red Buttons. "You feel *so safe*. And isn't that really what you want?" Lured to the wilderness to escape the dangers of secular civilization. What a paradox! But now it's time for fun. No one ever works at Sunset Village or Vanity Fair. There the motto reads, "A place to start living when you stop working." These are the early retired adults, business types who have put in their quarter-century of riding the rods on the Long Island Railroad and are ready now to take their matronly spouses out of the terror of divorce and into the trauma of idleness, the better to enjoy their menopause together.

See all those men and women—painting by numbers, chalking up another minus-ten at shuffleboard, dealing each other another hand at pinochle, conquering the world at backgammon, ecstatic over success at Mah Jong or Yahtzee. And the best part is that there are no children to interfere! Just mature adults, doomed to the atrophy of leisure in abundance, condemned by choice to waltz away their most productive years to the soporific rhythms of a Lawrence Welk mentality.

Why, then, are these people laughing?

The imprisonment of the urban cliff-dweller and the sterility of life in a retirement community lead one to ask, "Is this the best that material prosperity has brought us? Either to be afraid for our lives or to be afraid of them?" In either case, we lock ourselves away from the real world, like Laura Wingfield in Tennessee Williams's play *The Glass Menagerie*, to play with little toys—mere *things* that bring us emotional security and easement from The Great Fear.

BEHAVIORISM

But the tentacles of secularism reach beyond things themselves to the very idea of man. At root, materialism's preoccupation with things points to a mechanistic view of human life—man as a consuming machine. Man can thus be reduced to a configuration no more complex than a sophisticated version of Karel Capek's robot, the better to explain his working parts. Love and learning, security and satisfaction can all be accounted for—as can their opposites, fear and frustration—as positive or negative mechanical responses to certain stimuli. Identifiable physical secretions, and even puzzling impulses whose source can only be inferred, eliminate any necessity to look beyond the limits of bodily functions for explanation. So say those to whom man is the human machine.

Unwilling to grant the human being properties such as mind, spirit, or soul—except perhaps as unsatisfactory metaphors—this kind of Secular Man reduces all human thought to mere "behavior." J. B. Watson, a founding father of behavioral psychology, claimed that "the behaviorist finds no mind in his laboratory, sees it nowhere in his subjects." Instead, for Watson and his followers, man became distinguishable as man—that is, different from other animals—because his behavior was observed to be different; human ideas became reality only when they were made observable as action.

Watson's latter-day successor as the guiding light of behaviorism is Professor B. F. Skinner of Harvard University. Originator of the "Skinnerian box" for conditioning laboratory animals, author of *Walden Two* and *Beyond Freedom and Dignity*, Skinner is the arch-opponent of those atavistic thinkers (in his view) who still persist in attributing to man such qualities as mind. "Mentalists" he calls them, and he sneers at their reactionary suggestion that such a phenomenon as consciousness should be thought to exist.

But Skinner dispenses not only with consciousness but also with conscience. "As we have seen," he writes in *Beyond Freedom and Dignity*,

> man is not a moral animal in the sense of possessing a special trait or virtue; he has built a kind of social environment which induces him to behave in moral ways.

Thus Skinner passes off any notion of the moral or immoral nature of humanity; he moves then to his higher aim, what C. S. Lewis called "the abolition of man." Skinner claims,

> His abolition has long been overdue. . . . To man *qua* man we readily say good riddance. Only by dispossessing him can we turn to the real causes of human behavior. Only then can we turn from the inferred to the observed, from the miraculous to the natural, from the inaccessible to the manipulable.

Skinner's quarrel is with what he calls "autonomous man"—the human being whose mind and will Skinner's antagonists choose to infer from conscious acts of choice. Such an antagonist is Professor Brand Blanshard of Yale University. In a debate with Skinner, Blanshard concludes that behaviorism leaves a vacuum at the heart of our moral and practical life. It makes us out to be hollow men in a wasteland. It tells us that we are machines—enormously complicated machines, but in the end nothing more. Let us assume for the moment that this is true, and ask what would be the value of a world in which only such machines existed and that unscientific embarrassment, consciousness, did not exist. The answer I suggest is simple: it would have no value at all. Consciousness, however frail and evanescent, is the seat of all goods and evils, of all values of all kinds, and they would go out with it like a candle.

Skinner finds no cause for distress in the extinction of the candle of consciousness, for the notion of consciousness is to him an *ignis fatuus*, a false light. He is far more troubled by the use of terms such as "good" and "evil," which he finds irrelevant and outmoded. The behaviorist prefers instead to speak of "efficient" or "inefficient" reinforcements to behavior or means of changing a person's behavior. Such changes become, in his jargon, "behavioral modifications," and they may be achieved through repetition stimulated by reward or pain; through reorientation assisted by hypnosis, propaganda, or other forms of brainwashing; through drugs and even through surgery. All of these techniques have as their goal the modifying of natural biological urges toward mere individuality, which the behaviorist takes to be antisocial behavior leading to the dangerous possibility of anarchy.

To support his claims that all cognitive, affective, and psychomotor processes can be explained by the rubric of stimulus-and-response, the mechanistic behaviorist points to his statistics. This obsession with the measurement of everything is the fruit, in John Leonard's phrase, of "scientism rampant." To a definition of art such as the poet Emily Dickinson once referred, the psychometrician counters with equations and delta ratios. Dickinson said, "If I read a book and it makes my whole body so cold no fire can ever warm me, I know *that* is poetry." But to the behaviorist looking to fill his charts and graphs with verification, the chill through the spine, the gleam in the eye, has no validity. Such subjectivity, he will argue, is nothing more than the uttering of unutterable sublimities, wild gyrations of language essentially meaningless because unmeasurable.

The same is true of moral values. The Ten Commandments, a meeting of the American Psychological Association was told by its president Donald T. Campbell, may have been useful in modifying primitive natural urges towards independence; for that reason, the Ten Commandments might well be studied in that light rather than dismissed as superstitious taboos. But Campbell is almost alone among prominent psychologists in suggesting that traditional moral values have any interest for societies today. More often, the question of moral values is shrugged off in cultural snobbery. What, after all, are moral values? Which moral values? Whose moral values? By what standard are we to judge? The behaviorist prefers to localize any discussion of morality to conventions in a given society.

Fascinated by measurement, the behaviorist's favorite question is *How much?* Never *Why?* Perhaps even more puzzling to his mechanical view of life is this refinement of the question: *Why and with such infinite variety?* For it's this human capriciousness, the personal and unpredictable assertion of will, that most confounds and dismays behavioral psychology. Why are some human beings more often loving than cruel? Why can the same human being become cruel only an instant after having acted lovingly? Norman Carlsen, director of the Federal Bureau of Prisons, has said, "We don't know what causes crime in this country. The behaviorists haven't told us." And why not? Because the behaviorists don't know!

But behaviorists do know what they expect from human beings. More than anything else, they want order and uniformity. They want the absolute reliability of the models in their laboratories. In *Where the Wasteland Ends*, Theodore Roszak describes behaviorism's predilection for the mechanical as "a distaste for the unruliness of human ways, a mania for system, centralization, control." He goes on to point out, in searing and prophetic terms, what he sees as the political direction of such control: "It is toward the programmed society, the republic of automatons."

In his satirical novel, *That Hideous Strength*, C. S. Lewis gives one of his dehumanizing engineers this speech: "If Science is really given a free hand, it can now take over the human race and recondition it: make man a really efficient animal. If it doesn't— well, we're done." Lewis's apocalyptic portrayal of scientism rampant calls to mind two more appraisals: the ironic prophecy of Michael Young, *The Rise of the Meritocracy: 1870-2033*, which predicts a planned society built upon criteria of intelligence testing; and *Player Piano*, the 1952 novel by Kurt Vonnegut, Jr. Long before most of us had even heard of the Univac machine, Vonnegut anticipated the "military-industrial complex" and bureaucratic human engineering. Thirty years later, the Vietnam war fulfilled much of Vonnegut's prophecy, bringing into our homes the reality of computerized combat: a depersonalized launching of "smart bombs" and the blind assault of napalm upon villagers who— promulgators of military doublespeak told us—must be destroyed in order to be liberated. Now, once more, art anticipates human nature, as the motion picture *Star Wars* precedes an astral defense system. How long before the human engineers begin their campaign of behavior modification, preparing us to accommodate to this newest terror?

For some time artists have been warning us against the innocuous exterior presented by behavioral reductionists. A mechanized, cybernetic assumption of control over budgets— the school district, the municipality, at first—leads readily to decision-making with regard to legislation and the supervision of life-supporting professions. And this is only a preliminary step to behaviorism's ultimate goal: the bondage of the whole person to predetermined controls—as Skinner would say, beyond human freedom, beyond personal dignity. In a remarkable appendix, Roszak catalogues a few declarations by behavioral spokesmen under these telling headlines: "The Automization of Personality," "Therapy by Terror," and "The Nihilism of the New Biology."

To catch a further glimpse of the behaviorist's dream, one need only hear anthropologists and students of primate life discussing the future. At the Yerkes Institute, a Federal research facility in Atlanta, Georgia, behavioral psychologists today conduct their experiments on apes and chimpanzees. But if, in fact, the purpose of such experimentation is to transfer its findings to human behavior; and if it can be argued that human beings are really only human animals; and if so, it can be established that experimentation carried out on primary subjects is both more efficient and more productive, then the next step is obvious. Novelists have been suggesting this grotesque possibility for many years—Aldous Huxley's *Brave New World* and Anthony Burgess's *A Clockwork Orange* are only two examples. But at the death camps of the Third Reich, we saw the earliest practical utilization of surgical experimentation to achieve behavioral modification of human beings. The same curse continues, Aleksandr Solzhenitsyn assures us, in the Soviet gulag prison systems. And, lest we be too eager to accuse others, recent investigations of the Central Intelligence Agency's illegal activities have disclosed the use of powerful drugs to achieve that Agency's purposes.

These barbarous acts, of course, reveal only one of the dreadful extremes toward which secularism may lead. B. F. Skinner, Jose Delgado, Jacques Monod, and other human reductionists aren't viciously pursuing the liquidation of the human race. Their intentions are quite the opposite. They see the terrifying prospect of trying to cope with life on our overcrowded, underfed planet. Together with management specialists and human engineers, they're searching for some efficient accommodation to the new conditions of life facing us in the twenty-first century.

One of these concerned seers is Garrett Hardin, an early proponent of "lifeboat ethics"—the calculated decision to let some people die in order to save the rest—a form of benevolent genocide. Another word becoming popular among advocates of Hardin's theory is *triage*, a term borrowed from the World War I practice of selecting certain wounded to receive the limited medical assistance available, while leaving others to recover or not, as their condition allowed.

Another spokesman is Jay Forrester, professor of management at the Massachusetts Institute of Technology. Concerning the crisis he argues,

> We are at a point now where we must give up the idea
> that good is good in the ideal sense and realize that
> what is good now may be bad in the future.

The solution Forrester proposes is to limit agricultural exports, thereby affecting population growth. Another way of saying it would be to starve the poorer nations to death.

To help us decide the difference between our ideal sense and the long-range future practicality, we shall be herded together into what O. W. Markley of the Stanford Research Institute calls "a managed society ruled by a faceless and widely dispersed complex of warfare-welfare-industrial-communications-police bureaucracies with a technocratic ideology." Another name for such an existence may be Hell.

There we may find toward what purpose mechanistic behaviorism is pushing us. Skinner declares boldly, "Its goal is the destruction of mystery."

The Unknown, the Inscrutable, the Imponderable, the Eternal Question still baffles Secular Man, leaving him to stumble in his inadequacy, dizzied by the ridiculousness of his posturing. He can no longer endure being borne along on a wave of feckless optimism, only to see himself, time after time, driven against the rocks of reality. He must *know* who he is, his reason for existence, his destiny. Now even the grudging resignation of William Ernest Henley's "Invictus" seems outdated and futile:

It matters not how strait the gate,
How charged with punishments the scroll,
I am the master of my fate;
I am the captain of my soul.

Instead, Secular Man more often sees himself as King Lear describes Edgar, "Unaccommodated man . . . a poor, bare, forked animal." And in this knowledge he seeks for consolation.

SECULAR HUMANISM

But secularism, like the monster Hydra of Greek mythology, has many heads, many faces. Some bear remarkable likeness to each other; some stand as bitter antagonists. The more benign behavioral psychologist, for example, may have much in common with the biologist who recognizes that, whatever else mankind may be, the human race is responsible, accountable to each other and to history, for the quality of all life on this planet. This commitment to responsibility, however individually defined, often forms the basis of ethical humanism, sometimes called secular humanism.

Before proceeding, I must attempt to insure that the reader recognizes the inherent differences between humanist philosophies. Not all humanism is either secular or ethical humanism; there is also Christian humanism. Far from being a contradiction in terms, Christian humanism is what the gospel is all about—the blending of Christian belief with human experience, a fusion of faith and action, devotion to Christ walking hand-in-hand with everyday business. Christian humanism, as practiced by Martin Luther, John Calvin, Desiderius Erasmus, Thomas More in the sixteenth century—as demonstrated by T. S. Eliot and Dag Hammarskjöld, by Charles Malik and Mother Teresa in this century—exemplifies what it means truly to love the Lord our God with heart, soul, strength, and mind. Christian humanism rejoices in the fact of the Incarnation, by which God invests himself in the fullness of human experience, its joys and disappointments, its triumphs and losses, its love and betrayal. Christian humanism makes the angels yearn to trade places with us who know both the spiritual and physical dimensions of God's love. But Christian humanism is not mere humanism, for the essence of Christian humanism is a recognition of the human condition, our sinful and stubborn hearts estranged from God until wooed and won back by Jesus Christ's love.

Not so the ethical or secular humanist, for whom the idea of sin as part of the human condition is unacceptable. To the ethical or secular humanist, sin is no more than "anti-social behavior," while evil is an aberration found only in madmen like Adolph Hitler or the Ayatollah Khomeini. Instead, the ethical or secular humanist is unceasingly optimistic about the essential goodness of human beings, stalwart in the face of today's newspaper headlines. "The Peace Corps needs you to fix up the world" reads a recruiting poster: this appears to represent ethical humanism's highest ideals. The New York Society for Ethical Culture advertises its Sunday school—"Tuition, $80 for the first child, $30 for each additional child"—in this sanguine certainty:

> So You Want Your Child to be an Ethical Person, to Care About People and Justice?
>
> Our Sunday School Can Help You! Ethics is Our Religious Commitment.

Ethical humanism contests any assumption that man lacks sufficient inner resources to improve himself or the character of society. Its thesis is the statement by Protagoras, "Man is the measure of all things." A leading spokesman for ethical humanism in this century has been the American man of letters, Joseph Wood Krutch. His book, *The Measure of Man*, rises as a testimony to his belief in the essential grandeur of the human race. It is also a declaration of war against dehumanizing materialism and reduction of man to a machine. Krutch wrote,

> Perhaps Hamlet was nearer right than Pavlov. Perhaps the exclamation "How like a God!" is actu-

ally more appropriate than "How like a dog! How like a rat! How like a machine!" Perhaps we have been deluded by the fact that the methods employed for the study of man have been for the most part those originally devised for the study of machines or the study of rats, and are capable, therefore, of detecting and measuring only those characteristics which the three do have in common. But we have already gone a long way on the contrary assumption, and we take it more completely for granted than we sometimes realize. The road back is not an easy one.

To begin this long road back to human freedom and dignity, the ethical humanist opens by reasserting the existence of man's phenomenal advantage over animals, the uniqueness of *mind*. Mind is the quality denied by reductionists and only begrudgingly acknowledged by humanistic biologists, such as the late J. Bronowski, who noted amusedly that there must be some difference between Skinner and his laboratory animals, "or else," said Bronowski, "they would be studying Skinner."

Various humanistic explanations are offered, from natural evolutionary progression to inexplicable evolutionary accident. Some anthropologists suggest that during the aeons of human development, *homo sapiens*, acting upon the impulse of will, exchanged certain physical attributes—the prehensile tail, for example—for mental powers. As preference for thought increased and the need to hang by one's tail decreased, so the brain enlarged and the tail atrophied. All this came about, of course, as the result of an unquenchable act of the human will energized by the newly evolving human mind.

So, humanistic biologists, unable to account for the origin of either mind or will, are left to concede, with the late Sir Julian Huxley, that "man is of immense significance" if only because

he is a reminder of the existence, here and there in the quantitative vastness of cosmic matter and its energy equivalents, of a trend toward mind, with its accompaniment of quality and richness of existence.

In other words, the attestation to man's uniqueness is not to be found in enzymes or skull measurement; nor in dispute over the presence of soul or spirit. Instead such proof is to be discovered in "a trend toward mind"—the development through cultural evolution of fire and the wheel, of videotape and pocket calculators.

Such reasoning, it would seem, verges dangerously close to a return to materialism. It begs the question of origins by leaping to the observable things man can produce to prove his power. Thus the tension remains between two conflicting secular philosophies. One exists solely at the level of the material, the lowest possible scale on Plato's twice-bisected line, a slave to sense experience. The other assumes a posture contemptuous of material sense experience, holding—without being able to prove— that the unaided human reason is sufficient to perceive reality.

This is the glory of ethical humanism: its delight in man made in his own image. At its highest, secular humanism considers ethical problems to be within the purview of the mind because, it says, moral ideas are innate. While denying the existence of any absolute values, the ethical humanist contends that truth, goodness, honor, and justice, along with all other virtues, exist relatively and can be exemplified in any man. H. J. Blackburn, formerly director of the British Humanist Association, says, "The humanist does not believe that there is a universal good for man, or a purpose that determines his destiny. He is on his own and has to discover by experience what is good, each for himself within his own culture."

As a theory, secular humanism sounds appealing. But what of experience? History shows that, without recognition of a universal moral Good, man readily assumes that what satisfies *his* lusts and indulges *his* pride may logically be called "good." Furthermore, observation of social behavior teaches us that all too often what is "good" for generic man turns out to be equally bad for the other half of the human race—woman.

In many parts of the world the heaviest labor not performed by machine or animal is done by woman. Tiny Nepali women are found on the highway to Kathmandu before sunrise hauling heavy timbers strapped to their backs by headbands. In South India, shriveled Tamil women bear on their heads loads of firewood and carry them for ten miles and more; these burdens are too heavy for a lone man to lift, yet every afternoon the road to Kodaikanal market is lined with women porters.

Along the principal highway in Bangladesh, a Muslim husband walks ahead of his family. Behind him a few paces are his wife and small children clinging to her sari; she carries a wicker hamper on her head and an infant in her arms. Her husband is empty-handed. He shouts at her to hurry up, and a few moments later, displeased at her continuing slow pace, picks up a stone and hurls it at her.

Where is the evidence for an innate ethical concern for human values? The catalogue of atrocities committed by supposedly civilized peoples in the name of "national interest" comprises an appalling condemnation of secular humanism's relative moral code. Even if limited to a very few events in this century, the list is too shameful for belief. Tsarist pogroms upon the Jews of Russia begin the wretched index, followed by England's savagery upon the Boers of South Africa; Stalin's purges murdering millions of his fellow-countrymen; Fascism's onslaught against Spain; American paranoia and chauvinism in the relocation of 100,000 American-Japanese citizens to concentration camps in 1942; Pope Pius XII's decision to ignore the existence of the German campaign to exterminate Europe's Jews; the needless destruction of Dresden in 1945, followed by the mushroom clouds over Hiroshima and Nagasaki; Nigeria's enforced starvation of thousands in Biafra; the systematic slaughtering of Bengalis by Pakistani troops; Idi Amin's crazy liquidation of whole tribes; the Chinese "cultural revolution" and its chaos for 800 million people; Iran's heartless holding of American hostages; the butchering of helpless victims by suicidal terrorists; continuing apartheid in South Africa.

How shallow the mere listing of these crimes against our fellowmen! How profound the humanist misconception of mankind's essential goodness! For now common sense renders "*ethical* humanism" a misnomer. By its dependence upon the supposedly innate and rational persuasions of right and wrong, humanism exposes its ignorance of human nature. Relying solely upon its own criterion for Good—the power of human reason—secular humanism rejects any revelation of objective standards of righteousness, such as may be claimed in the Bible to be the demands of a just and holy God. Instead, the humanist resorts to solipsism, the notion that the self and only the self matters since one cannot be judged apart from one's own standards.

This is a satisfying doctrine to Secular Man, who may not recognize one of its chief exponents to be Shakespeare's notorious scoundrel Polonius—corrupt politician, faithless father, and spouter of platitudes wholly in keeping with his character:

> This above all, to thine own self be true,
> And it must follow, as the night the day,
> Thou canst not then be false to any man.

Yet by his own example, Polonius inverts his ethics. False to both his son Laertes and daughter Ophelia, false to his rightful king and prince, Polonius is true to himself only when deceiving another.

Most secular humanists aspire to rise above Polonius' tawdry example. Yet secular humanism is powerless to effect the ideals it urges. Theodore Roszak strikes home when he says,

> Humanism, for all its ethical protest, will not and cannot shift the quality of consciousness in our society; it has not the necessary psychic leverage. Indeed, it stands full square upon the stone that must be overturned. After all, the reductionists who see nature as a machine and the human being as a robot are not apt to regard moral indignation as anything more than a queer quirk in the robot's electro-bio-psycho-chemico-physical feedback apparatus. And who are the humanists to talk to them of the reality of soul or spirit?

We shouldn't be surprised, therefore, at moral failure in a secular humanist society; especially, we shouldn't be surprised in image-conscious America, where what counts about people is what appears, not what is. We don't concern ourselves with persons but with impressions. "That's why I thank Almighty God you're both built like Adonises," Willy Loman the Salesman tells his sons. "Because the man who makes an appearance in the business world, the man who creates personal interest, is the man who gets ahead."

To get ahead. *To make it*. This is the secular dream. The values of secular humanism may be seen every weekday, from noon to late afternoon, in the domestic dramas we laughingly call soap operas: "The Guiding Light," "As the World Turns," and "All My Children," for instance. But these shows are far more serious than many of us realize, for not only do they impel their more bizarre fanatics to cry or send wedding gifts and funeral wreaths to fictitious characters; these programs also prescribe the secular ideal for The Good Life: a home in the suburbs, a husband who is a doctor or lawyer, and the unfailing cup of coffee with a neighbor whose ethical concern offers the only panacea to frustration and heartache. The soap opera heroine—and by extension her daily, real-life companions—inhabits a totally secularized environment. Yet it is an environment grown arid and stale. The very titles of the series say so: "The Young and the Restless," "Search for Tomorrow," "Days of Our Lives," "Another World," "One Life to Live." There is no God in Soap Opera America; no one bothers to ask the source of the Guiding Light or where one may find the still point of the turning world.

In this quagmire of relative values, ethical humanism continues to call for moral rectitude and human compassion. Unfortunately, the motives behind apparent probity and charity may be less than genuine. Some time ago, the magazine *Newsweek* sponsored an occasional display advertisement in its own pages. This full-page ad comprised *Newsweek*'s "Responsibility Series," published (so a footnote told the reader) "with the hope

it will remind some Americans of their basic responsibilities."
One of these homilies was called "The Incorruptible Man."

> If he's in the District Attorney's office, the word
> quickly spreads, *"No deals."*
>
> If he is in a key position to sign contracts, the ad-
> vice is, *"Don't tamper."*
>
> If he is sent alligator shoes, tickets to Paris, or a
> suspicious-looking, bulging envelope, *"He'll send
> them back."*
>
> His presence gives society a solid counterbalance
> to a contemporary who may be allergic to what a
> Chief Justice called, "The Sea of Ethics."
>
> Without him, civilizations collapse.
>
> What a clean, powerful, satisfying, psychological
> edge you have, if, in your field of endeavor, the In-
> corruptible Man is known as *you!*

No doubt, the writer of this advertisement for decency had
good intentions. Like the rest of us, he prefers a society free
from corruption. But his message, at first cloyingly sentimental,
turns sour when its true import becomes clear: "Be honest," he
says, "because it will give you an advantage—an *edge*—over
your competitors." According to the secular creed, even integrity is a weapon, to be used by those who think they possess it.

When we discover that we ourselves have been the victims
of opportunist ethics, as in the infamous Watergate and related
scandals, then we find it difficult not to gag upon reading the
pious rhetoric of Richard M. Nixon's Second Inaugural Address:

> To a crisis of the spirit we need an answer of the
> spirit. And to find that answer, we need only look
> within ourselves.

As every honest person will admit, it's not enough to "look
within ourselves," for when we do, we find disclosed the
fraudulence of secular humanism. To look within ourselves
means that, with Hamlet's mother Gertrude, we find "such

black and grained spots/As will not leave their tinct." That look within may only confirm what we have long suspected: that moral decay is endemic in human society. If so, aren't we then left to ask, with T. S. Eliot, "After such knowledge, what forgiveness?"

For the generation that remembers the assassination of John F. Kennedy as its baptism into the ways of the world, political scandal may simply serve as further proof that what Os Guinness calls "the dust of death" has settled like a pall on everything they know. Every material object, every appeal to reason seems coated by cynicism and betrayal. Yet negativism in itself is no solution; it doesn't fill the void. A substitute must be found, and the most ready substitute has frequently been the drug experience and the fugitive fellowship it brings. But here again, in every case, the fraudulence of narcotic bliss makes itself plain—or ends in physical death.

Increasingly, therefore, a more benign substitute presents itself in the guise of absorbing personal relationships called by a variety of terms—"sensitivity training," "reality therapy," "self-actualization," "encounter therapy," "communal marriage," "the Esalen experience"—and known generically as "the Human Potential Movement." The one-time spokesman for youthful rebellion and anarchy, Jerry Rubin, describes his pilgrimage from Yippie guru to Yuppie in a three-piece suit. In a single five-year period, Rubin confesses,

> I directly experienced est, gestalt therapy, jogging, health foods, tai chi, Esalen, hypnotism, modern dance, meditation, Silva Mind Control, Arica, acupuncture, sex therapy, Reichian therapy, and More House—a smorgasbord course in the New Consciousness.

Yet Peter Marin sees humanistic cults as the ironic opposite of their claims to bring mankind together. In his view, these various therapies exemplify "the new narcissism" in which "the self replaces community." Marin writes,

What is lost is the immense middle ground of human community. The web of reciprocity and relation is broken. The world diminishes. The felt presence of the other disappears, and with it a part of our own existence.

Why? Why do supposedly intelligent young adults submit themselves to brainwashing, to mouthing the platitudes of subservience to a "perfect master," to paying out large sums of money for weekend instruction in "astral projection"? The answer isn't hard to discover. In spite of all they have been told— by behavioral scientists, by social statisticians, by psychometricians, by pollsters and computerized dating services—young people today refuse to accept the nonexistence of reality beyond a time-space continuum. They're drawn irresistibly to believe in that other dimension so long withheld from them, the realm of spiritual reality.

For some, their quest has led into the jungles of satanism, voodoo, and the occult; for others, there has been a fleeting taste of the diluted *Godspell* of Jesus Christ the Superstar. Still others look for satisfaction in the vapid innocence of Nature Boy or the 1960's "Flower-Child" syndrome. But in all these directions, secular humanism leaves a person to be victimized by naivete because the premise of secular humanism ignores human evil as a fact of life. It provides no defense against selfishness, deceit, and rage; it must end in a morass of frustration and despair, even in neurosis or suicide. So, are the consequences of commitment to secular humanism any less tragic than to materialism or mechanistic behaviorism? The exaltation of man, grounded upon nothing more stable than blind belief in the goodness of human nature, is as lethal as cyanide. For in a society in which every moral virtue is held only in relation to its ethical context, disillusionment cannot be far away.

This disillusionment burst open in 1973, splitting America like an earthquake's abyss, swallowing up the most powerful man in the world and a score of his followers. Richard Nixon and the men fallen with him were strong-willed, self-righteous men in whose conduct we had brought before us, in startling detail, the tragedy of secularism in modern culture.

All the components were present: the materialist's preoccupation with cash and security, with sophisticated inventions amorally used, and ultimately, with a satisfaction procured through the amassing of absolute power; the mechanistic obsession with control of human behavior through social stimuli programmed to engineer a conditioned response from the electorate; the opportunist's appeal to any means to achieve desired ends in defense of a self-serving ideology; and most poignantly, the humanist's blindness to the fact that what held the team together was loyalty to a captain and a game-plan designed to subvert the rules.

We listened in astonishment to lies from the highest office. We heard ingenuous statements by petty functionaries who could not realize that they had been betrayed by the very men whom they had hoped to serve. One of these explained his actions this way: "Somewhere between my ambition and my ideals, I lost my ethical compass."

HEDONISM

Under the stress of human turpitude and disappointment, secular humanism seems doomed to fail. A person may then feel confronted by two remaining alternatives: either to make the best of the absurd human predicament or accept the likelihood of human annihilation. Choice determines consequences, whether laughter in the face of absurdity or despair at the probability of extinction.

The modern spokesman for endurance in the face of absurdity is the French novelist and Nobel Prize winner Albert Camus. Against the mindless optimism of fools, Camus sets forth the reality of man's predicament as he sees it.

> It happens that the stage sets collapse. Rising, street-car, four hours at the office or the factory, meal, streetcar, four hours of work, meal, sleep, and

Monday Tuesday Wednesday Thursday Friday and Saturday according to the same rhythm—this path is easily followed most of the time. But one day the "why" arises and everything begins in that weariness tinged with amazement.

The question is "Why?" The answer, "For no purpose—unless, perhaps, to ask the question." Camus considers such questioning healthy because it marks the rise of anxiety in the human consciousness, and Camus agrees with Martin Heidegger, that anxiety is "at the source of everything." So Camus congratulates the young man who notices the passing of his thirtieth birthday.

He admits that he stands at a certain point on a curve that he acknowledges having to travel to its end. He belongs to time, and by the horror that seizes him, he recognizes his worst enemy. Tomorrow, he was longing for tomorrow, whereas everything in him ought to reject it.

To signify man's condition and offer an example to emulate, Camus provides his "absurd hero," the Greek mythological figure of Sisyphus. Doomed in the Underworld forever to push a rock to the top of a hill, only to see it roll each time to the bottom, Sisyphus epitomizes every man, says Camus, whose "whole being is exerted toward accomplishing nothing." But Sisyphus pauses to watch his stone fall back downhill, and for Camus it is Sisyphus's grim determination that interests him most. "I see that man going back down with a heavy yet measured step toward the torment of which he will never know the end." In his acceptance, "he is superior to his fate. He is stronger than his rock."

Perhaps—although Camus does not say—Sisyphus also laughs as he descends his hill—laughs at the meaninglessness of his endeavor, laughs at the very fact that his laughter defeats the gods who punish him, laughs even at himself. In his laughter the absurd man asserts his inner freedom, for Camus does allow that "there is no fate that cannot be surmounted by scorn." Laughter, therefore, may well seem the only sane response to absurdity; and in a vacuum of meaninglessness, the pursuit of pleasure may appear to be life's only worthwhile objective.

To pursue pleasure is to be a hedonist. The word *hedonism* derives from the Greek words for pleasure and sweetness. One of the early philosophers to teach the ethics of hedonism was Epicurus (341-270 B.C.), his teachings we know as Epicureanism. One of the first principles of Epicurus is that

> we declare pleasure to be the beginning and end of the blessed life; for we recognize this to be our first and natural good, and from this we start in every choice and avoidance; and this we make our goal, using feeling as the canon by which we judge every good.

Historically speaking, there is surely a valid distinction between ancient Epicureanism and the grosser forms of hedonism in modern culture. The idealism of Epicurus called for responsibility in human actions because, he said, "it is not possible to live pleasantly without living wisely and well and righteously." But according to the third-century anthologist, Diogenes Laertius, who devoted an entire volume of his *Lives and Opinions of the Famous Philosophers* to Epicurus, the definition of *good* rose no higher than mere sensation:

> I know not how to conceive the good apart from the pleasures of taste, sexual pleasures, the pleasures of sound, and the pleasures of beautiful form.

Later followers of Epicurus tried to elevate his ethics into a search for the *summum bonum*, "the greatest good of the greatest number," as the English philosopher Jeremy Bentham expressed it in 1789. From Bentham came the philosophy of utilitarianism, later developed by John Stuart Mill in the nineteenth century. Bentham presupposed a fluctuating standard for *utility*, which he called "that property in any object whereby it tends to produce pleasure, good, or happiness, or to prevent the happening of mischief, pain, evil, or happiness to the party whose interest is considered."

Here the final phrase is important: "the party whose interest is considered." One scarcely needs to be a scholar of the history of ideas to see a relationship between Epicurus, Bentham, and the latter-day proponents of "situation ethics." A whole generation of youth has grown to maturity suckled on the theories of Joseph Fletcher, William Sloan Coffin, Jr., and other relativistic wet nurses. Whatever is good for you, provided it doesn't harm anyone else, is good.

But like so many other humanistic prophets crying in the wilderness, Epicurus has developed a sore throat. His message has been distorted and reduced to an epigram: "If it feels good, it is good." A full-page advertisement announcing a sexy motion picture redefines hedonism in our secular culture:

> Nothing is wrong if it feels good. . . . Sensuality is
> a part of life, and it should be a part of your life, too.
> A wonderful, beautiful part. It's time for all of us to
> say that nothing is wrong if it feels good.

A fitting metaphor for the new hedonism might be an amusement park with its concessions, daredevil rides, and games of chance. The sole purpose in spending one's time and money at Great Adventure is to enter wholly into a realm devoted to unending pleasure. Nourished by mores as evanescent as cotton candy, the perpetual pleasure-seeker wanders the midway from one entertainment to another—from the grotesqueries of a freak show to the titillation of burlesque and beyond. Spun to dizziness by whirligigs, cheated by pitchmen, the hedonist, like a child at a carnival, laughs his way to the next trumpery.

What's more, the hedonist knows what he's doing. He makes no pretense of arriving at any permanent satisfaction. He knows the flatness of life when its effervescence has evaporated, its stale aftertaste. He knows the anticlimax expressed in the song,

Is that all there is?
Is that all there is?
If that's all there is, my friend,
Then let's keep dancing,
Let's break out the booze and have a ball. . . .

Perhaps a better analogy for the hedonist view of life is the bacchanalia, a feast given by Trimalchio. In Albert Camus's novel *The Fall*, his narrator Jean-Baptiste Clamence describes his riotous life:

> I was at ease in everything, to be sure, but at the same time satisfied with nothing. Each joy made me desire another. I went from festivity to festivity. On occasion I danced for nights on end, ever madder about people and life. At times, late on those nights when the dancing, the slight intoxication, my wild enthusiasm, everyone's violent unrestraint would fill me with a tired and overwhelmed rapture, it would seem to me—at the breaking point of fatigue and for a second's flash—that at last I understood the secret of creatures and of the world. But my fatigue would disappear the next day, and with it the secret; I would rush forth anew. I ran on like that, always heaped with favors, never satiated, without knowing where to stop, until the day—until the evening rather when the music stopped and the lights went out. The gay party at which I had been so happy . . .

The ellipsis is Camus's dramatic way of showing how the voice of Jean-Baptiste Clamence drifts off in momentary introspection. He knows—and his honesty compels him to admit—that the party must always come to an end.

Another novel, F. Scott Fitzgerald's *The Great Gatsby*, provides an enduring commentary on the hedonistic life. The novel's episodic structure carries the reader from one party to another—a dinner for four, an assignation to which spectators are invited, an extravagant divertissement recorded in Fitzgerald's technicolor style:

By seven o'clock the orchestra has arrived, no thin five-piece affair, but a whole pitful of oboes and trombones and saxophones and viols and cornets and piccolos, and low and high drums. The last swimmers have come in from the beach now and are dressing upstairs; the cars from New York are parked five deep in the drive, and already the halls and salons and verandas are gaudy with primary colors, and hair bobbed in strange new ways, and shawls beyond the dreams of Castile. The bar is in full swing, and floating rounds of cocktails permeate the garden outside, until the air is alive with chatter and laughter, and casual innuendo and introductions forgotten on the spot, and enthusiastic meetings between women who never knew each other's names.

The lights grow brighter as the earth lurches away from the sun, and now the orchestra is playing yellow cocktail music, and the opera of voices pitches a key higher. Laughter is easier minute by minute, spilled with prodigality, tipped out at a cheerful word. The groups change more swiftly, swell with new arrivals, dissolve and form in the same breath; already there are wanderers, confident girls who weave here and there among the stouter and more stable, become for a sharp, joyous moment the center of a group, and then, excited with triumph, glide on through the sea change of faces and voices and color under the constantly changing light.

Suddenly one of these gypsies, in trembling opal, seizes a cocktail out of the air, dumps it down for courage and moving her hands like Frisco, dances out alone on the canvas platform. A momentary hush; the orchestra leader varies his rhythm obligingly for her, and there is a burst of chatter as the erroneous news goes around that she is Gilda Gray's understudy from the Follies. The party has begun.

At such a party, as everywhere else in hedonism, the only rule is that there are no rules. Camus's Jean-Baptiste Clamence knows this and declares, "The essential is being able to permit oneself everything." This is the philosophy of satisfying the pleasure principle. Under its tenets, the hedonist boasts of a freedom withheld from the more timid. "I never care what I do," claims Lucille, a habitue of Gatsby's weekends, "so I always have a good time."

As if in echo, the actress Valerie Perrine tells reporter Judy Klemesrud of *The New York Times*,

> I don't care if I act as a sex symbol. Personally, I like sex, and I don't care what a man thinks of me, as long as I get what I want from him—which is usually sex.

"True debauchery," says Camus's narrator in *The Fall*, "is liberating because it creates no obligations. In it you possess only yourself; hence it remains the favorite pastime of the great lovers of their own person."

The hedonist is also searching for variety, for quantity rather than quality in his experiences. What appears as promiscuity to a moralist is only novelty to the hedonist, in adherence to Camus's dictum in *The Myth of Sisyphus*:

> If I convince myself that this life has no other aspect than that of the absurd, . . . then I must say that what counts is not the best living but the most living. It is not up to me to wonder if this is vulgar or revolting, elegant or deplorable.

So, it is no longer the *summum bonum* for which the hedonist strives but the *summus numerus*, the greatest number of thrills, of conquests, of world's records for self-indulgence. A smorgasbord table has always been the glutton's delight.

But a novel like *The Great Gatsby* also tells a larger truth about the consequences of living in a world of gluttony and narcissism, wholly given to pleasure-stroking and self-gratification.

For when the party is over, the narrator Nick Carraway gives his impressions of its aftermath. Looking across from his house to Gatsby's mansion next door, Nick observes that

> a sudden emptiness seemed to flow now from the windows and the great doors, endowing with complete isolation the figure of the host, who stood on the porch, his hand up in a formal gesture of farewell.

Later, Nick imagines

> a night scene by El Greco: a hundred houses, at once conventional and grotesque, crouching under a sullen, overhanging sky and a lusterless moon. In the foreground four solemn men in dress suits are walking along the sidewalk with a stretcher on which lies a drunken woman in a white evening dress. Her hand, which dangles over the side, sparkles cold with jewels. Gravely the men turn in at a house—the wrong house. But no one knows the woman's name, and no one cares.

One of the consequences of hedonism may be an abysmal inner loneliness resulting from an emphasis solely upon self. Hedonism's highest goal is the attainment of exclusive, personal satisfaction, whatever the cost to others. In time, this essential selfishness must alienate every hedonist from his companions; and so, the gyro of pleasure-seeking, the endless round of party-going, must turn ever more inward, spiraling always toward total egocentricity. Spiritual and emotional vertigo is at last hedonism's only legacy.

In Ernest Hemingway's *A Farewell to Arms*, another self-confessing hedonist, Frederick Henry, rejects an invitation from a quiet-living priest to visit his peasant village. In prose pulsating with wretchedness, Hemingway shows the alternative chosen by his narrator.

I had gone to no such place but to the smoke of cafes and nights when the room whirled and you needed to look at the wall to make it stop, nights in bed, drunk, when you knew that that was all there was, and the strange excitement of waking and not knowing who it was with you, and the world all unreal in the dark and so exciting that you must resume again unknowing and not caring in the night, sure that this was all and all and all and not caring.

The theme of carelessness is hedonism's leitmotif: "I don't care . . . no one cares." But here hedonism is brought face to face with its own grim paradox. For in the supposed freedom claimed by those who "don't care" lies bondage to meaninglessness. If no one cares what I do, it must be because what I do isn't worth caring about; essentially without merit, without value, without meaning. An awareness that my actions have no consequence to anyone, including myself, is unsettling.

To counteract this affront to his personal worth, Secular Man must adopt some means to force from his fellows the recognition he needs. In other words, if not approbation, then at least an expression of outrage. Anything will do; but the hedonist must know that he matters to somebody. So he often revels in silly exhibitionism.

When private indulgence becomes too commonplace and drab, the next advance can only be to strip away that privacy; in the language of militant homosexuality, "to come out of the closet." Thus an alliance of homosexuals and lesbians, once fearful of society's disapproval and reprisals, marches boldly up a New York City thoroughfare, proclaiming "Gay Liberation." One of its advocates, Michael F. Valente, a professor of religious studies at Seton Hall University and author of *Sex: The Radical View of a Catholic Theologian*, takes to the soapbox on *The New York Times* Op-Ed page. His message? The corollary he finds between homosexuality and a gourmet's taste for escargots.

Notoriety for its own sake becomes the norm. Plastic

dolls—from rock singers and actresses to athletes and social-
ites—vie with each other to become cynosures of scorn. Scandalous drunkards and drug addicts, reprehensible parents, nym-
phomaniacs and womanizers become drained of their moral dignity as persons. Avaricious publicity agents, like lamprey eels,
suck from them the last vestiges of character, leaving them as
soulless zombies. In *Wired*, his biography of the self-
destructive entertainer John Belushi, journalist Bob Woodward
recounts how those dependent on Belushi's continuing popular
success supplied him with cocaine and other drugs to keep him
in his manic frenzy as performing clown. Woodward writes,

> Giving or selling drugs to John was a kind of game,
> like feeding popcorn to the seals at the zoo; give him
> a little and he would perform, be crazy and outrage-
> ous; a little more and he'd stay up all night, outdanc-
> ing, outdoing, outlasting everyone around him. . . .
>   John needed psychiatric help, and [a Chicago psy-
> chiatrist] offered to see him professionally. "You've
> got to get him off drugs," he said deliberately [to
> Belushi's producer]. "If you don't, get as many
> movies out of him as possible, because he has only
> two to three years to live."

The psychiatrist was right. Less than three years later, Belushi was dead, another of those whom Dante would consign to
the Second Circle of his Inferno, men and women who had "betrayed reason to their appetite."

For pleasure-seekers still too cautious to expose themselves to social opprobrium, there's always the vicarious thrill
of voyeurism, the masturbating eyeball, and the fantasy of identification with a celebrity less inhibited. Here one may think first
of the steamy newsstand publications with their pretensions to
eros rampant in centerfold photographic spreads. But any mature browser in such pornography will quickly observe how
juvenile their eroticism is. For sexual stimulus, it follows well
behind a corpse on the embalmer's slab. The models, both male

and female, are seldom aroused nor arousing; they are little more than clinical studies in limp flesh. Mannequins in a department store window are more lifelike.

By far more seductive are the appeals pandering to self-gratification in the full-page advertisements. By inference, the reader is led to assume that using this particular deodorant brings the promise of owning a Georgian mansion with semi-circular drive and a Jaguar XKE. Drinking that brand of scotch makes a man eligible for another fistful of creature comforts. Wearing clothes by a certain designer guarantees a manner of living concomitant with the company of rich and beautiful women.

For a period of pleasure-induced narcosis, all may be well, as Malcolm Muggeridge recalls:

> Contrary to what is often suggested, a hedonistic way of life, if you have the temperament for it and can earn a living at it, is perfectly feasible. The earth's sounds and smells and colors are very sweet; human love brings golden hours; the mind at work gives great delight.

Under the continuing influence of the Serpent's secular lie, "You will not die; you will be like gods," hedonism flies even in the face of mortal reality—expiration, rigor mortis, decomposition. To any rationalist daring to question his categories, the hedonist gives this stock reply in laughter: "It can't happen to me, but if it does, so what?"

But can any truly thinking person go on endlessly pursuing phantoms? At some point he must stop to ponder the point of it all. "There are certain queer times and occasions," writes Herman Melville in *Moby-Dick*,

> in this strange mixed affair we call life when a man takes this whole universe for a vast practical joke, though the wit thereof he but dimly discerns, and more than suspects that the joke is at nobody's expense but his own.

No intelligent hedonist can survive without this ironic self-awareness. Only stepping back and, through objective distance thus obtained, scrutinizing oneself can keep the mind in balance. But after such withdrawal, after a refocusing of perspectives gone awry, is laughter any longer an appropriate response? Laughter at oneself has its limits; thereafter, those hollow reverberations frighten one to death.

Life is no laughing matter. Mark Twain alleged that "the secret source of Humor is not joy but sorrow," and in *Moby-Dick* Melville condemned as insincere or immature the foolish seeking for joy in sensuality. His second mate aboard the Pequod is Stubb, a rollicking sailor whose dying words are a call for liquor and sex. Meditating earlier upon this disproportion of values, Melville writes, "So, therefore, that mortal man who hath more of joy than sorrow in him, that mortal man cannot be true— not true, or undeveloped." Then a literary parallel:

> With books the same. The truest of all men was the Man of Sorrows, and the truest of all books is Solomon's, and Ecclesiastes is the fine hammered steel of woe, "All is vanity." *All*.

The Speaker (or Preacher) of Ecclesiastes may have been one of the foremost hedonists in history—one of Camus's record-breakers. A king, an inordinately wealthy man, a scholar, he nonetheless turned away from matters of state and economics, from science and philosophy, to follow after pleasure. He attempted to satisfy his physical appetites through rich foods, fine wines, and a thousand women. Finding these insufficient, he turned to aesthetics—architecture, landscaping, music, dance, sport. His conclusion, reached after the full hedonistic experience, is unqualified negation:

> "Laughter," I said, "is foolish. And what does pleasure accomplish?". . . everything was meaningless, a chasing after the wind; nothing was gained under the sun.
>
> (Ecclesiastes 2:2, 11)

A modern analogue to Ecclesiastes is Hemingway's novel *The Sun Also Rises*, which title comes from Ecclesiastes 1:5. In this novel Hemingway exposes some of the emptiness behind the facade of gaiety, noise, constant motion, drunkenness, indiscriminate sex, and whatever else purports to bring pleasure. At the novel's end, the narrator Jake Barnes, sexually and symbolically impotent, rides through Madrid with Lady Brett Ashley, a moral vagrant. "Oh, Jake," Brett cries, "we could have had such a damned good time together." Jake replies—is he listless, sardonic, or despairing?—"Yes. Isn't it pretty to think so?"

NIHILISM

But we no longer live in the Roaring Twenties, and the Lost Generation, with its childish hedonism, scarcely belongs to any serious attempt at characterizing our age. We are more than disenchanted expatriates. We are sojourners in interplanetary space, governed not by Ptolemy's understanding that our realm is the center of the universe but by a post-Copernican realization—a sense of lostness in space so empty, so menacing. As we contemplate the vastness of the void into which we stare, we may well be transfixed by its inscrutability so that we ask, with Melville's Ishmael, what meaning—if any—may be found anywhere in the universe.

> Is it that by its indefiniteness it shadows forth the heartless voids and immensities of the universe, and thus stabs us from behind with the thought of annihilation, when beholding the white depths of the milky way? Or is it . . . for these reasons that there is such a dumb blankness, full of meaning, in a wide landscape of snows—a colorless, all-color of atheism from which we shrink?

To all these questions, there is but one secular answer, and that must be given by the nihilist, whose philosophy is literally a belief in *nothing-ism*. The term "nihilist" was first popularly used by the Russian novelist Ivan Turgenev in 1861. He applied it to Bazarov, the central character in his novel *Fathers and Sons*, whose radical social philosophy held that all existing institutions were corrupt and must be overthrown. Annihilation was the only means of redemption.

Nihilism is an attitude of ultimate despair, the notion that nothing matters because nothing really is. The most extreme formulations of this teaching have been developed in our own generation, but nihilism is far from a new philosophy. The Speaker of Ecclesiastes expressed as well as any modern nihilist the totality of his despair:

"Meaningless! Meaningless!"
    says the Teacher.
"Utterly meaningless!
    Everything is meaningless."
What does man gain from all his labor
    at which he toils under the sun?
        . . . .

For with much wisdom comes much sorrow;
    the more knowledge, the more grief.
        . . . .

Man's fate is like that of the animals; the same fate
awaits them both: As one dies, so dies the other. All
have the same breath; man has no advantage over the
animal. Everything is meaningless. . . .
And I declared that the dead,
    who had already died,
are happier than the living,
    who are still alive.
But better than both
    is he who has not yet been,
who has not seen the evil
    that is done under the sun.
        . . . .

So my heart began to despair over all my toilsome
labor under the sun. (From Ecclesiastes 1-4)

In modern philosophy, Martin Heidegger is responsible for articulating the human experience with Nothing (*Nichtung*). Our sense of dread or *Angst*, he says, transcends mere anxiety or fear, which are always related to anxiety *over* something or fear *of* someone. Instead, Heidegger claims, the dread that must be faced is nameless, indefinite, inscrutable; thereby it reveals the Nothing and our lapse into total abandonment. This we must accept and draw ourselves into stoic resolution against flinching. Whatever our fate, we are alone and must accept it with dignity. Nihilism stems from an aggravated sense of futility, outrage at the accidental circumstance called life. Nihilism grinds its teeth at an admitted impotence in dealing with inexorable realities, such as the inevitability of death. To be sure, there would appear to be sound reasons for a growing nihilism today. Ironically, some of these causes may be related to a surging, if temporary, backlash against secularized living—its materialism, its mechanized depersonalization, its wasteful indulgence. The development in our time of nuclear fission, of miniaturization and rocketry, increase alarmingly both man's capability of and propensity for destroying the human race. Destruction doesn't have to come about through evil premeditation. It could be simply the result of a technological blunder. So, once again, The Great Fear intrudes.

The advent of such fearsome power scares us into looking for other hidden dangers. Suddenly we are aware that we have been monsters in the playpen, throwing over the slats of our world toys meant to amuse, food and drink meant to nourish. This realization comes too late in some instances; already certain natural resources have been exploited beyond any hope of replenishing. Imminent and long-range prospect of disease and plague—the result of our having fouled our own nest—torments us. The land we live on, the water we drink, the air we breathe bear evidence of scandalous indifference to the needs of humankind. Ironically, as we have recently discovered, in the cosmetic preoccupation of perfuming our armpits with aerosol deodorants, we may be permanently contaminating the ozone content on which we depend for life.

But internal reasons far more compelling may also predispose Secular Man toward nihilism. One may read Friedrich Nietzsche's parable of the madman who lit his lantern at high noon and went running to the marketplace, looking for God. When his tormentors ridiculed his search, the madman turned to them and said, "God is dead. God remains dead. And we have killed him." But this famous parable doesn't end there. For the madman goes on to explain that his mission has been premature, his audience unprepared for his message.

> This tremendous event is still on its way, still travelling—it has not yet reached the ears of men. . . . This deed is still more distant from them than the most distant stars—and yet they have done it themselves.

The nihilist, therefore, sees himself as one ahead of his time. He has discerned the message of the madman. He reads Dostoevski: "If God did not exist, everything would be permitted." He reads Jean-Paul Sartre: "Everything is indeed permitted if God does not exist, and man is in consequence forlorn, for he cannot find anything to depend upon either within or outside himself. . . . That is what I mean when I say that man is condemned to be free."

But here a useful distinction needs to be made between nihilism and existentialism as it is popularly understood: the existentialism associated with the names of Sartre, Camus, and others. Sartre is sometimes linked with nihilism, perhaps by those who misconstrue the title of his book, *Being and Nothingness*, assuming it to be an apology for nihilism. It is not. Sartre's existentialism presumes existence—being or is-ness. His famous slogan, "Existence before essence," gives priority to being, and Camus says, "The point is to live."

But not merely "to live"; rather, the existentialists aligned with Sartre would argue, to live freely and with the consequences of choice. In *Existentialism and Humanism*, Sartre wrote, "I am thus responsible for myself and for all men, and I am creating a certain image of man as I would have him to be.

In fashioning myself I fashion man." So speaks a professing atheistic existentialist, but he does not carry the whole existentialist argument. In fact, the forerunner of modern existentialist thought, Søren Kierkegaard, shows how deeply existentialism may be rooted in a dynamic Christian faith. In his journal Kierkegaard wrote,

> The most tremendous thing which has been granted to man is: the choice, freedom. And if you desire to save it and preserve it there is only one way: in the very same second unconditionally and in complete resignation to give it back to God, and yourself with it.

Here, then, is a fundamental difference between existentialism and nihilism. Whereas existentialism may or may not accept the existence of God as the irreducible absolute of reality, nihilism's first assertion must be atheism—the denial of absolute reality anywhere. Once a conception of God—the *sine qua non* of belief in being—has been eliminated, it takes no great philosophical gymnastics to achieve a leap into the void of nothingness. No God means no Creator; hence, no creation or creature, no Creator's image in which that creature may be shaped; no human nature to mirror the *imago dei*. In his unfinished allegory, *The Mysterious Stranger*, Mark Twain gives Satan the nihilist creed to express to mankind:

> There is no God, no universe, no human race, no earthly life, no heaven, no hell. It is all a dream—a grotesque and foolish dream. Nothing exists but you. And you are but a thought, a homeless thought, wandering forlorn among the empty eternities.

The nihilist feels abandoned, but he can't yield to that intimation of abandonment for fear of conceding the existence of the Abandoner. The result is often a consuming rage, futile in the face of such vast uncaringness. Simone Weil tells of a beggar who said to Talleyrand, "Sir, I must live," to which Talleyrand replied, "I do not see the necessity for that." And the desperate Stephen Crane, choking on his own consumptive breath, characterized man's impotence in this poem:

> A man said to the universe:
> "Sir, I exist!"
> "However," replied the universe,
> "The fact has not created in me
> A sense of obligation."

For the Nobel Prize-winning biochemist, Jacques Monod, man's only option is to accept "the fundamental postulate that there is no plan, that there is no intention in the universe." The cold consequences, according to Monod, will then be man's final realization that

> like a gypsy, he lives on the boundary of an alien world. A world that is deaf to his music, just as indifferent to his hopes as it is to his suffering or his crimes.

In order to come to terms with life, the nihilist accepts a maddening atheism. The effect is dizzying, a sickness far worse than physical, since atheism compels the contradiction of thinking about what doesn't exist. The idea of God, says Nietzsche's Zarathustra, "makes all that is straight crooked and all that stands giddy." To think about God is "vertigo to the human frame, and vomiting to the stomach." Disorientation to life often shows itself in an impoverished imagination, a spirit sick almost unto death. "There is an inescapable sense," writes Barbara Rose, "among artists and critics that we are at the end of our rope, culturally speaking." The reason for cultural despair is not merely that the avant-garde artist has run out of ideas. It is, instead, that creation without a Creator has left him in a devalued economy, morally and imaginatively bankrupt. To cope with the universe he inhabits, the nihilist artist must cheapen its worth even more, denying the value of permanence and heightening the inflation of trivia.

But the foremost problem facing the nihilist is one of language. It is impossible to speak of Nothing in a conceptual vacuum. Nothing can only be the negative opposite of Something. How then can Something be said not to exist? The very shape that Nothing fills was formed by Something. And so the wordplay goes round and round. To speak of nihilism becomes a contradiction in terms, just as to make a claim for atheism may be, at root, a compensatory and begrudging acknowledgment of God. The nihilist may wish, as Karl Heim says, to affirm an expression of himself that is "positive and world-accepting" rather than negative and suicidal. Yet, he finds, to predicate his world-and-life view upon a denial of existence, he must stand upon the very ground he denies.

Perhaps this is why so many nihilists choose action and the nonverbal arts to make that affirmation. The motion picture director Roman Polanski, influenced perhaps by the senseless slaughter of his wife Sharon Tate by Charles Manson's banshees, has given his philosophy in dark and brooding films. Asked to sum it up, he needed but eight words: "We are born, it means nothing, we die."

Much of the art of our time expresses Polanski's quiet desperation. But some is aggressive in its contempt for life. At the Whitney Museum on New York City's upper Madison Avenue, an exhibition by Lucas Samaras offers picture frames reversed and hanging so that the back of the canvas shows. Plunging through each canvas is a twisted, rusted knife, as if the unseen painting had been stabbed from the front.

In *Future Shock*, Alvin Toffler sees a relationship between psychological and social instability and "the impulse toward transience in art." He cites the "happening," a brainchild of Allan Kaprow in the 1950s, as an indicator of meaninglessness within our society. "The happening," says Toffler, "is the Kleenex tissue of art."

One of Kaprow's "happenings" is called *Self-Service*. Intended to be performed in New York, Boston, and Los Angeles during the summer of 1966, it consisted of some of the following acts, quoted from Kaprow's published script:

NEW YORK

On the shoulder of a stretch of highway a fancy banquet table is laid out, food in the plates, money in the saucers. Everything left there.

People stand on bridges, on street corners, watch cars pass. After two hundred red ones, they leave.

An empty house. Nails are hammered halfway into all surfaces of rooms, house is locked, hammerers go away.

Couples make love in hotel rooms. Before they check out, they cover everything with large sheets of black plastic film.

Rockets, spread over several miles, go up in red smoke, explode, scatter thousands of scraps of paper with messages.

On the streets, kids give paper flowers to people with pleasant faces.

Couples kiss in the midst of the world, go on.

People shout in subway just before getting off, leave immediately.

Warehouse or dump of used refrigerators. People bring packages of ice, transistor radios, and put them into the boxes. Radios are turned on, refrigerator doors are shut, people leave. On another day they return, sit inside with radios for a while, and quietly listen.

Everyone watches for either: a signal from someone
a light to go on in a
window
a plane to pass di-
rectly overhead
an insect to land
nearby
three motorcycles to
barrel past.

Immediately afterwards, they write a careful description of the occurrence, and mail copies to each other.

Kaprow's instructions to participants in this event concluded by saying, "There will be no rehearsals and the work will not be repeated."

Beyond Kaprow are the conceptualists. At their purest, these artists contend that the *objet d'art* is irrelevant; only the idea matters, the critical frame of mind in which art is conceived. At its most ludicrous, an exhibition of conceptual art becomes a non-event, as when Robert Barry shut down his Amsterdam showplace and posted a sign, "For the exhibition, the gallery will be closed," while Michael Heizer demolished a parking area outside the Berne museum where his work had been displayed. To other conceptualists, a telephone call, a face-to-face conversation, a videotape of some transitory occurrence—these are works of art. The more ephemeral, the more nearly intangible, the better.

But not all conceptualists are benign idealists. Some are destructive; some evince behavior vicious and masochistic, with overtones certainly suicidal if not genocidal. Most are also mercenary. On 4 July 1975, a San Francisco group of conceptual artists known as the Ant Hill staged an old-fashioned "happening" in the parking lot of the Cow Palace arena. They burned television sets, they drove a Cadillac into the rubble to smash symbols of bourgeois culture. All the while their own videotape equipment and cameras of television networks recorded the "Media Burn." And the conceptualist sold souvenir T-shirts for five dollars each.

In Vienna, Rudolf Schwarzkogler, beginning with his penis, literally amputated himself to death. In Los Angeles, Chris Burden has been shot with a .22 rifle, crucified to the roof of a Volkswagen van, and has crawled over broken glass—all for the benefit of cameras recording these instances of conceptual art in books selling for eight hundred dollars.

There are even larger fees. In 1975, for example, Sol LeWitt's instructions for drawing a line on a wall sold for eight thousand dollars. Today, a former subway graffiti vandal can command twenty-five thousand to fifty thousand dollars for a canvas. Painters like Keith Haring, Jean Michel Basquiat, and David Salle can expect to make hundreds of thousands of dollars in a year's sales of their so-called "New Art." Crazy? Perhaps. But before we laugh too loudly, we do well to reflect a moment. The joke is obviously on those of us so thirsty for some taste of authenticity in a plastic desert, we will even pay to be ridiculed.

Perhaps the most faithful realization of conceptual art has been Piero Mangoni's exhibition in Milan: samples of his own feces labeled "*Mierda d'Artista*."

Undoubtedly, the most destructive merger of art and nihilism has been the rock music concert, brought home by means of televised programming. "Music videos" now occupy 24-hour cable systems, as well as network showtime. Yet how few parents, in particular, seem able to grasp the lethal effect upon their children of a steady diet of angry noise and clenched fist. They seem not to understand the maniacal devotion many of these alleged musicians demonstrate—an undisguised allegiance to death. Thus many parents, along with others—teachers, psychologists, social workers—fail to comprehend how rock music videos, with their lurid depicting of anarchy and despair, help seduce young people into suicide by making death appear attractive.

Under the influence of this violent and nihilistic mentality, art representing us takes on more and more the shape of our spiritually famished souls. William Barrett has said it strikingly in his book, *Irrational Man*:

> There is a painful irony in the new image of man that is emerging, however fragmentarily, from the art of our time. An observer from another planet might well be struck by the disparity between the enormous power which our age has concentrated in its external life and the inner poverty which our art seeks to ex-

pose to view. This is, after all, the age that has discovered and harnessed atomic energy, that has made airplanes that fly faster than the sun, and that will, in a few years (perhaps in a few months) have atomic-powered planes which can fly through outer space and not need to return to mother earth for weeks. What cannot man do!

But Barrett's exclamation is ironic, for he goes on to say,

He has greater power now than Prometheus or Icarus or any of those daring mythical heroes who were later to succumb to the disaster of pride. But if an observer from Mars were to turn his attention from these external appurtenances of power to the shape of man as revealed in our novels, plays, painting, and sculpture, he would find there a creature full of holes and gaps, faceless, riddled with doubts and negations, starkly finite.

The Swedish poet Harry Edmund Martinson, in his epic *Aniara*, reverses Barrett's visit from outer space, taking Secular Man on his ultimate one-way flight to Nothingness. Martinson's poem is, perhaps, without equal as a testament to secularism's "inner emptiness." Published in 1956, before the first Sputnik rekindled mankind's interest in erecting a new Tower of Babel, *Aniara* tells the story of a sorrow-laden interplanetary vehicle, a refugee ship from stricken Earth to Mars, a spaceship now lost forever in galactic gloom.

Aniara's plot is simple. Poisoned by repeated warfare, Earth has been rendered uninhabitable. To escape, survivors of the Thirty-Second World War emigrate to Mars on huge spaceships, measuring three miles long and a half-mile wide, each carrying thousands of passengers. The poem is a personal log of that voyage, kept by an engineer responsible for the care of a godlike computer called the Mima. This wonder possesses attributes of omniscience and compassion; its purpose is to entertain Earth's orphans as they journey to their new homeland.

But disaster overtakes the spaceship named Aniara when a near-collision with an asteroid causes the ship to swerve out of its course. Missing the orbit of Mars, Aniara's captain then attempts to steer toward some other refuge known to our galaxy. But hostile meteors and other forces prevent the earthship from succeeding, until at last the narrator laments, "we'd passed the point of no return." Bound now for a galaxy fifteen thousand light years away, the narrator resigns himself to his doom.

His only consolation is the Mima, now revered as a female deity. For several years the computer-goddess devotes herself to comforting those who, in despair, prostrate themselves before her shrine. Her screens project vistas of unknowable rapture somewhere in the cosmos, causing occasional glimmers of hope. But these soon become even more futile than the sexual orgies to which the emigrants resort, frenzied, goaded by rhythms of remorse, conscious that they are lost.

When the Mima can no longer withstand cruel reality, she destroys herself, taking with her exploding psycho-mechanism the last illusions of rescue for those now eternally marooned. Earth's displaced persons, bereft of the Mima, turn back to more primitive religions—the Cult of the Vagina, the Sect of Ticklers—to rid their minds of gnawing fear.

During the long years of this ill-fated passage, the narrator begins to realize that there is no way to "shut out the intolerable void," both without and within himself. Outside the interplanetary omnibus yawns an immensity unfathomable to the human mind: through its "gaping gorges" rush all the pent-up shock waves of evil, forever imprisoning our galaxy and corroding human aspirations. Even so, the broad expanse without is no match, he says, for those gulfs and chasms within, "a void/which must be constantly filled and embellished." The narrator also begins to understand that "no one can hide his inner emptiness."

The truth, hinted at from the beginning of the poem, now crashes in upon the narrator as he approaches his end. He comprehends the futility of technological and mechanistic theory and looks beyond the laws of the Zodiac in hopes of finding another gospel. In keeping with literary conventions of the epic, the narrator has the right to pass on his experience to later generations: he has not forgotten entirely the ageless cosmic promise of Good News—the coming of a hero-redeemer whose love heals the heart of its loneliness.

THE SECULAR WASTELAND

Secularism in all its forms has run amok through our world-culture. It leaves in its wake devastation of the country-side and dismembering of human beings; the cruel pollution of our planet and that "inner emptiness" of men's souls. Left alone to face the grimness of the Unknown, Secular Man has no means to satisfy the farthest ranges of condition, the deepest fathoms of need; no way to measure forlorn tundras of ego-space; no way of crossing frozen glaciers of doubt; no hope of avoiding the eternal graveyard of disbelief. Nothing but what Karl Heim describes as

> a cry for help thrown out at some forlorn point of the world's immeasurable night, in the midst of an in-finitude containing only rolling masses of matter, a cry which rends the air for a moment within an insig-nificant radius about its place of origin, to be swal-lowed up next moment in the icy-silence of world-space and lost.

Such a cry for help comes, for example, in the poignant lyrics of a contemporary song,

> May I return to the beginning,
> The light is dimming and the dream is too.
> The world and I, we are still waiting,
> Still hesitating. Any dream will do.

Yet even in the moment of conscious need, a shameless refusal to admit the truth—that most dreams dissolve into delusion or nightmare—keeps secular men and women wandering in the wilderness of their own design.

In 1922, T. S. Eliot described the sterility of life in "The Waste Land." Near the end he wrote,

> What are the roots that clutch, what branches grow
> Out of this stony rubbish? Son of man,
> You cannot say, or guess, for you know only
> A heap of broken images, where the sun beats,
> And the dead tree gives no shelter, the crickets no
> relief,
> And the dry stone no sound of water . . .
>
> If there were the sound of water only
> Not the cicada
> And dry grass singing
> But the sound of water over a rock
> Where the hermit-thrush sings in the pine trees
> Drip drop drip drop drop drop drop
> But there is no water.

In the arid secular culture there can never be springs of living water. Secularism's resources are no better, Eliot says, than "voices singing out of empty cisterns and exhausted wells." The poet is recalling words of the prophet.

> They have forsaken me,
>   the spring of living water,
> and have dug their own cisterns,
>   broken cisterns that cannot hold water.
>
> (Jeremiah 2:13)

If men and women today would quench their thirst, they must find an alternative to the cracked cisterns of secularism.

Chapter 3

Scarecrows in a Melon Patch: The Seduction of Idolatry

*M*ircea Eliade defines the secular or nonreligious man as one "who accepts only a profane existence, divested of all religious presuppositions." Because of new global technology and the secular attitudes it engenders, Secular Man appears to have succeeded in desacralizing himself, ridding himself of whatever lingering superstitions he may have held concerning God, the soul, or any quaint notions of life-after-death. Set free from fear of angels or demons, Secular Man can concentrate upon eluding the modern Furies that pursue him—what E. V. Hill calls "a lotta isms that oughta be wasms!"

Daily the assumptions of secularism seem to grow, numbing society against questioning its presuppositions. Yet even so, a surprisingly large number of people—including many not professing the Christian view of a universe lovingly created and redeemed—seem to agree that secularism is a dead-end street. In fact, if secularism has any potent opposition in our worldwide culture today, that opposition comes not so much from Christians as from practitioners of other faiths.

Of course, even some secularists are willing to admit the

need for some means of rooting out the world's evil and establishing a utopia on earth. An editorial in *The New York Times* expresses this latent longing:

> Surely this is the time of the year when Eve persuaded Adam to eat the fruit, there in Eden. . . . There is a sense of new, more profound knowledge, if one will only go and seek; of new, more perceptive answers, if one will only propound the questions; of new Edens beyond the blue-misted hills. . . . Meanwhile, the apple is there to be eaten, and the gates of Eden are open to two-way travel.

Quite apart from its romantic distortion of the Genesis story, the sentiments of this editorial in a major international newspaper, suggest a fundamental human need. Discontentment haunts the inner being of every man and woman, a vacuum meant, apparently, to be filled by a power greater than ourselves. No one lives and dies entirely free from this troubling dependence. Each of us needs Something or Someone to worship. Until we are filled, we are incomplete persons, possessed by an inner emptiness and subject to the vandalism of transient lusts and insatiable desires.

The most earnest attempts to rid ourselves of this void within have always been religious—an effort to recognize benign purposefulness to the universe and thus to our own existence; to combat theories of indeterminacy and randomness governing our destinies. Rudolf Otto, in 1917, presented Europe with a book translated into English as *The Idea of the Holy*. There Otto postulated the universality of religious emotion in what he identified as the numinous and described the holy God as being "wholly other."

Before and since Otto, philosophers and theologians have spoken of religions as being either "revealed" or "natural." Revealed religion requires objective support of history to elevate it above merely visionary and subjective cults. Judaism, Christianity, and Islam are the world's principal revealed religions, each claiming revelation through historical persons and their scriptures—the Law and the Prophets, the Old and New Testaments, the Qur'an.

Natural religion, on the other hand, treats with suspicion any formulation of creed limiting its adherent to a single, allegedly "revealed" means of access to truth. The statement of Jesus, for example, disqualifies him before natural religion as a narrow-minded bigot: "I am the way. . . . No one comes to the Father except through me" (John 14:6). Natural religion is inclusive, allowing varieties of persuasion where Judaism, Christianity, and Islam are categorical. The Hindu, for instance, reads in his Bhagavad Gita, "Whatever god a man worships, it is I who answer the prayer." The Jew, the Christian, the Muslim rejects Vishnu's inclusiveness, taking quite literally the First Commandment given to Moses and Israel: "You shall have no other gods before me" (Exodus 20:3).

To Jews, Christians, and Muslims, violation of the First Commandment is *idolatry*, a word inseparable from pejorative connotations. Granted, one man's idolatry may be another man's devout religion. But from the vantage of monotheism, devotion is not the criterion. Worship of any god or gods other than Yahweh, the Lord, Allah, is condemned. Not because idolatry is an ignorant alternative to the worship of One God; rather, because idolatry is a conscious rejection of eternal, cosmic truth. Some secularists would still dispute Otto's claim that religious awareness is common, without exception, to all rational human beings; but the burden of proof rests with them. Christians are convinced that God is that Being wholly other, known to all men by intuition at least, and known by revelation to all who diligently seek him.

Many ancient writings, the Genesis account among them, point to a time when one God was acknowledged by humanity. Scholars of comparative religion such as Mircea Eliade have documented the claim that polytheism is a later corruption of monotheism and not the opposite, as sometimes assumed. In the Genesis record, of course, God's original dealings commence with the creature made in his image, a single man named Adam. Through him—the priest ordained to tend the garden of God—

God chose to mediate knowledge of himself to Adam's race. But Adam's disobedience altered the plan of God and extended that mediation to other selected individuals. In the aeons before the Flood, all men knew how to invoke the Lord by name, although by what name we aren't told in Genesis 4:26. To Enoch, Lamech, and the peoples of their antediluvian epoch, a personal Idea of the Holy was a present reality in their lives—to walk with God, as Enoch did, or to rebel against him.

After Adam's failure, mankind's continuing rebellion required God to work his will through a wider structure, through Noah and his sons. But their descendants also failed to honor the Lord of the rainbow covenant; instead, the men of Shinar committed an act of hubris at Babel. Erecting their ziggurat testifies to their denial of the Other—an egoistic assertion of self by man, his thrusting upwards on the sole strength of what he can do. His objective was to make a name for himself, to rob God of his glory. This is the secular rejection of dependence upon a transcendent deity in preference for bricks and mortar and the technology of that time. The Tower of Babel is the first secular cathedral; its constructors, idolaters of self.

God chose next to make himself known to humanity through an entire nation, the children of Israel, the seed of Abraham. But even in the process of fulfilling his singular covenant with Abraham, God introduced him to powerful truth. From Ur of the Chaldees, across the Fertile Crescent, to the land of Canaan, Abraham had journeyed in faith's response to the summons of God. There he discovered the mysterious Melchizedek, king of Salem, living personification of a great truth, that God has never failed to make himself known to individuals regardless of nation or culture. For as Genesis 14:18-19 states, Melchizedek was "priest of God Most High, and he blessed Abram, saying,

'Blessed be Abram by God Most High,
    Creator of heaven and earth.
And blessed be God Most High,
    who delivered your enemies into your hand.'"

From his meeting with Melchizedek, Abraham had confirmed for himself that the Lord who had first appeared to him in his own country and among his own people was a universal God—the God of blessing and promise, the God of cursing and judgment, the Lord who had brought him from Ur to Canaan and now promised to make of him a great nation. He would later come to know this God, whose sign of dedication was circumcision, as Yahweh, and as Jehovah the Provider. But from Melchizedek he first learned to praise the Lord as Creator.

While God was working out his covenant with the generations of Abraham, Isaac, Jacob, and Joseph, no specific prohibition against idolatry appears to have been issued. None was needed. We read instead of altars built to honor the Lord and places named to commemorate an encounter with God. But there is no record that any of Abraham's family ever attempted to reduce the transcendent God of their father in fact and in faith to an icon like those of the people around them. Even the Egyptian concubine Hagar knew a name for God, whom she called "El-roi," meaning "God of a vision." To be sure, Jacob's father-in-law Laban had household gods, which his daughter Rachel stole from him. But this was so patently foolish to her husband, who had dreamed at Bethel and wrestled at Peniel, that Jacob's order to discard the foreign gods can only be regarded as common sense.

But by the time of Israel's deliverance from Egypt, all this had changed. Obviously the period of slavery in Egypt had adulterated Israel's worship of One God. After the mighty wonders of the plagues leading up to the Passover and the climactic parting of the Red Sea, the Lord declared an end to idolatry. Especially to be avoided was worship of the Canaanites' baals, variously revered as gods of weather, war, or fertility. From the beginnings of polytheism these had been sources of human dread—unpredictability of weather, ravages of war, failure to produce succeeding generations—to be appeased in many forms. Earliest, perhaps, were the fearful elements of nature, the unknown cause of light and darkness, thunder and lightning, rain, wind, and ultimately fire. But by giving each element a name, by personifying these powers and endowing them with human limitations and foibles, man sought to mitigate their anger and to ease his own fears. At Ur, the Chaldeans worshiped the moon god Nannar. The Sumerians' foremost deity was Ninurta, a god who like Zeus wielded the thunderbolt.

The ineluctable powers of nature are nearly an abstraction. No man can hold lightning in his hand or forestall the crash of thunder. But the effects of natural powers are often more concrete, and perceiving these effects brings humanity one step closer—so it was thought—to perceiving an unknown supremacy itself. It is much easier, therefore, to honor a rock formation, the result of wind and rain's erosion, than to worship wind and rain themselves. The configuration of stone thus takes on the shape of the Other, for by its very palpability it conveys attributes of timelessness and strength inherent in our most primary sense of deity.

After reverential awe for the elements of nature and their visible effects, develops the worship of other creatures in nature. Often such creatures appear to have instilled fear and loathing no less than some impending natural cataclysm. In other instances, they were as domestic as the Apis bull, worshiped by Egyptians and Canaanites thirty-five hundred years ago.

Frequently objects of idolatry have been subjects of the hunt, reverenced in their slaughter as well as in their mythic elusiveness. The caveman at Lascaux or Altamira may have drawn his pictures of bulls, horses, deer, and other animals as icons of universal archetypes; or he may simply have regarded them as inexplicable presences similar to those he was setting out to kill. We don't know. Scholars assume that some magical invocation may have accompanied the viewing of those remarkable paintings on the walls of prehistoric caves. Success in the hunt meant survival. Is it possible, therefore, that any hunter could have been so foolhardy as to embark on his quest for food and skins without first appealing to the sacred representations of the quarry he sought?

Early civilizations certainly seem to have adopted figures of animals, both real and imagined, as objects for incantation and ceremony prior to the hunt and, later, as symbolic mascots in war. The griffin, unicorn, sphinx, phoenix, and other mythic animals date back to earliest records of human society. In some Mediterranean cultures, for example, the griffin appeared as a symbol of authority or as a guardian of tombs. In these later representations, the creature also appears as an object of worship.

Pursuit of the beast in the field didn't eliminate the powers of the idol, whatever its shape. There remained always a sense of multiplicity and ubiquity, essential attributes of polytheistic deities. After all, weren't there still many bison remaining? Both those left alive and those brought back from the hunt must be related to that Other form from whose mystical being all bison receive their strength.

Some of these attitudes prevailed throughout the ancient Near East. But when the Israelites left Egypt, they were to set out on a great mission. As the Chosen People, they were called to be an example to the nations around them. No longer would Yahweh share his glory with gross representations in idol worship. Whatever earlier practices of idolatry had been allowed, these were now to be abolished; the original worship of the One True God was to be restored. Through Israel, mankind was to be reminded of what had long been forgotten. In *Saving the Appearances: A Study in Idolatry*, Owen Barfield writes,

> We shall understand the place of the Jews in the history of the earth, that is, of man as a whole, when we see the Children of Israel occupying the position in that history which memory occupies in the composition of an individual man.

Or, as Barfield goes on to say, the Jews were to become "the dawning memory in the human race."

They were to be "a peculiar people," calling back to mind the remembrance of God by asserting their cultural distinctives; separating themselves as the people of God from the rest of the nations. These distinctives were circumcision and a reverence for God's unutterable name, a word too holy for common and profane speech, a name to be spoken only by priests in worship. In his holiness, God is incapable of representation except as himself. He is I AM. In this disclosure, God summons unto himself all properties of being and essence. To attempt to represent any part of this divine whole becomes more than futile; it is an abominable offense against the One who Was and Is and Shall Be.

So the First Commandment given by the Lord through Moses declares "no other god." Its corollary is the Second Commandment:

> "You shall not make for yourself an idol in the form
> of anything in heaven above or on the earth be-
> neath or in the waters below. You shall not bow
> down to them or worship them; for I, the LORD
> your God, am a jealous God, punishing the chil-
> dren for the sin of the fathers to the third and
> fourth generation of those who hate me, but show-
> ing love to thousands who love me and keep my
> commandments" (Exodus 20:4-6).

These Commandments, says Owen Barfield, are "the unheard-of injunction."

> This is perhaps the *unlikeliest* thing that ever hap-
> pened. As far as we know, in every other nation at
> that time there prevailed unquestioned the participat-
> ing consciousness which apprehends the phenomena
> as representations and naturally expresses itself in
> making images. For the Jews, henceforward, any
> dealings with those nations were strictly forbidden.

From these special responsibilities accrued the continuing promises of the covenant: blessing for obedience, judgment for disobedience extending to the third and fourth generations. If this warning sounds like the threat of a vindictive God, petty in jealousy, unworthy of worship, the warning is also offered in loving concern. For the natural result of idolatry spills over from fathers to sons. It's a reckless bartering away of the original human birthright—spurned first by Adam, then by Cain, by Ham, by the men of Shinar, by Esau—the privilege of knowing and loving and serving the One True God. Idolatry is amnesia, forgetting God.

With such clear-cut alternatives, the profligacy of idol worship was proof to Israel's prophets of its manifest foolishness as a bogus religion. The transcendent God has revealed himself in personal dimensions throughout history. Idolatry therefore must be a quicksand of deceit, trapping men in dooming falsity. The prophet Jeremiah, for example, warned his fellow Israelites against becoming ensnared, like the pagan nations, in futile idolatry.

> Here what the LORD says to you, O house of Israel. This is what the LORD says:
>
> "Do not learn the ways of the nations
> or be terrified by signs in the sky,
> though the nations are terrified by them.
> For the customs of the peoples are worthless;
> they cut a tree out of the forest,
> and a craftsman shapes it with his chisel.
> They adorn it with silver and gold;
> they fasten it with hammer and nails
> so it will not totter.
> Like a scarecrow in a melon patch,
> their idols cannot speak;
> they must be carried
>   because they cannot walk.
> Do not fear them;
> they can do no harm
> nor can they do any good."
>
> (Jeremiah 10:1-5)

Jeremiah's condemnation of idolatry is, at least, rhetorically effective, dealing as it seems in cultural snobbery; it belittles pagan nations in their benighted polytheism. In Jeremiah's view, idolatry is a bunco game played by unscrupulous fakirs—a hoax that would be humorous, were it not so sad. So today, when a Westerner—perhaps a nominal believer in monotheism—thinks of idolatry, he may recall, first, the influences of primitive ancient religions upon his own culture: fertility rites, mystery cults, festivals honoring Osiris, Ashtoreth, Apollo, Aphrodite, Thor, and Odin.

Then he turns to the East and to impressions of exotic religious practices there. The gigantic obesity of a laughing Buddha towers over Taichung. In Mysore, the ferocious Hindu demon Mahisha grips a cobra in his right hand, while threatening with a scimitar overhead. In Papua New Guinea, a frightened animist clutches his talisman. In Malaysia, poisonous adders infest a Hindu temple and are venerated. And in Chittagong, Bangladesh, a Muslim sect scandalizes the orthodoxy of Islam. At the shrine Bayzid Bostami, a holy man is entombed and his remains displayed. But in a foul pond immediately in front of the shrine swim large and omnivorous turtles—possessors of the soul of the holy man. Even though idolatry is forbidden in Islam, a continuing stream of pilgrims visits the shrine, feeds the turtles to gain merit, while often ignoring the clusters of beggars who compete with the ravenous turtles for leftover scraps of food.

All scarecrows? Even the most chauvinistic Westerner must concede that, however benighted and superstitious, the pagan idolater is no fool. He too knows something about transcendence. He knows the difference between the sacred and the profane, as Mircea Eliade shows. Whether the idolater venerates a block of stone, a particular tree, a cheap plaster figurine, a shape carved by his own hands, or some form of animal life, Eliade says,

> what is involved is not a veneration of the stone in itself, a cult of the tree in itself. The sacred tree, the

sacred stone are not adored as stone or tree; they are worshiped precisely because they are *hierophanies*, because they show something that is no longer stone or tree but the sacred.

In these objects the pagan worshiper has identified something Other beyond the form itself. Sometimes this hierophany, to use Eliade's term, is verified to the pagan experience by evidence which the Christian finds both disconcerting and incontrovertible.

THE POWER OF PAGANISM

In February of each year, Hindus from the Tamil tradition participate in a festival of homage to their God of mercy, Lord Subramaniam. It's called Thaipusam. The three-day rite, attracting hundreds of thousands of faithful and curious, may be witnessed in Madurai, South India, and in Kuala Lumpur or Penang, Malaysia, where I saw Thaipusam celebrated.

On the first day, a silver chariot drawn by a team of sacred cows, duly draped and decorated for the occasion, carries a huge idol, almost a miniature temple in itself. This procession is accompanied by *chettiars*, pilgrims fulfilling acts of devotion and carrying consecrated coconuts to be smashed at intervals along the route of march. The idol is taken to a huge temple on Waterfall Road. Throughout the procession mothers attempt to have their young children daubed or splashed by the coconut milk, believing it to be blessed.

At dawn the next day, Thaipusam Day, February 6, a thousand devotees gather at various temples throughout the city of George Town, Penang. These men—a fifty-year-old father and his three sons, a twenty-eight-year-old named John Tan, an eighteen-year-old Chinese—are fulfilling vows of chastity and abstinence from food and alcohol for a thirty-day period. Now to complete their penance, they have promised to engage in a ritual that is its own version of the Via Dolorosa, a march along the Way of Sorrows. They're accompanied by friends and relatives who will serve like seconds at a duel, or handlers for a long-distance swimmer, to prevent the devotee from injuring himself or others.

For the fact is that when the pilgrim emerges from the temple to depart on his march of devotion, he is all but unaccountable for reasonable behavior. He's entranced, perhaps hypnotized, and bent upon but one objective—the ultimate payment of his vow in the Sri Bala Murugan temple in the hills above Waterfall Road. There he will learn whether or not his devotion has been accepted.

The Hindu believer comes forward to begin his march. He is barechested, wearing only a bright yellow *lungee* or wrap around his loins. But he carries with him the evidence of his earnestness, a *kavadi* or ornamental idol. It varies in appearance from man to man, but in essence each *kavadi* is a framework of light metal held overhead so that the representation of the god is elevated. Each *kavadi* is decorated with ribbon, crepe paper, flowers, and cloth streamers. From a distance the devotee appears to be wearing a birdcage over his head and torso.

But upon approaching the marchers, a grim realization strikes the observer. The bars of the so-called birdcage are a score and more metal lances projecting from the rim overhead and embedded in the bearer's chest and stomach. He is walking with spears in his body!

Behind him come several like him, their torsos encased by a webbing of rods like hunting arrows whose razor tips are sunk in human flesh.

Now another type of flagellant comes into view. Like the first, he is barechested except for a double row of fresh limes attached by hooks to his breast. Through each nostril, through both lips, through his eyelids, through his protruding and thickening tongue—a tiny barb. Running through his cheeks, a slim iron rod nearly ten feet long. A headband keeps his jaw from opening to tear his face apart; his hands grasp the spear tightly on either side of his face to keep the shaft from torquing.

All the way down the line of march, onlookers encourage the *kavadi* bearers, shouting "*Vel-Vel, Vel-Vel,*" just as spectators might cheer an Olympic marathon runner on his course. Concession stands sell trinkets and souvenirs of the occasion. Ice cream vendors hawk their wares. A cacophony of popular songs mixed with devotional hymns blares from competing loudspeakers. On every street corner Hindu sadhus, mendicant holy men, stand gazing steadfastly at the equatorial sun, their cheeks streaming with matter from their ruined eyes. Their alms cups are continually being filled by passersby seeking indulgences.

But here the procession has come to a momentary halt. One of the devotees, a young man impaled through the cheeks, is unaccountably withdrawing from the trance. His anguish is excruciating; his swollen tongue and fettered jaw make his pain unutterable. Before him comes a woman, evidently his mother, carrying a bucket of sacred coconut milk. Lovingly, yet sternly she exhorts him to take just one more step. As he does, she wipes his forehead with a cloth dipped in the milk, as if in reward. His suffering contorts every muscle, and his great toe stands erect as if in protest against further pain. But he goes on. The approval of the crowd reaches cascades of ecstasy.

I turn away, repelled at my own curiosity-seeking, but even as I do another group of *kavadi* bearers passes before me. These men don't carry the idol overhead; they pull it on crude carts made of a plywood flat and baby carriage wheels. These carts are attached to their bodies by yellow cords and steel hooks fastened into their backs.

The day is hot, nearly one hundred degrees Fahrenheit. At the point I see them, these pilgrims have struggled some four miles. They have another mile to go, much of it uphill.

Each *kavadi* bearer must leave the street and enter the precincts of the temple, where a frenzied throng awaits him. Along with other tourists, I follow the procession into the temple. Once inside the great doors, a blast of sound like a fire storm envelopes me. At the arrival of each devotee, the mob's cries of greeting reverberate with such deafening hollowness, I feel as though my own voice were being sucked out of me. I am overwhelmed by noise, by dissonance so powerful, so infernal, I feel almost swept away. For the first time I know for a certainty that I am a spiritual alien on hostile ground.

All that I have seen so far this day cannot begin to prepare me for what remains to be seen. For as I emerge from temple's dark enclosure into the midafternoon sunlight, the first *kavadi* bearers to complete their Thaipusam vows are returning from the hilltop temple. Back down Waterfall Road they come, passing the same crowds before whom they had toiled an hour earlier. But now they stride triumphantly, no longer burdened by the weight of the *kavadi*, no longer impeded by the spears and lances penetrating their bodies.

These instruments of death have all been removed and the spell broken by priests in the Sri Bala Murugan temple at the end of the march. Victorious, these supplicants of the Lord Subramaniam pass within arm's reach, carrying overhead, like a laurel wreath, the barbs and hooks of their humiliation. And on their tortured bodies there is no blood and there are no wounds.

No blood and no wounds!

The reality of this fact, so inconceivable yet so incontrovertible, attests a power beyond rational explanations. In the name of Lord Subramaniam, the god of mercy, believing Hindus have transcended the laws relating to flesh and steel— laws familiar to everyone who shaves. Beyond its bizarre public spectacle lie deeper reasons for such devotion. In 1945, a man named Sukuru was bayoneted in the right leg by Japanese soldiers occupying Penang. According to the local newspaper, *The Star*, the injury was permanent. "I underwent treatment in several hospitals but could not get well," Sukuru said. "My right leg was practically useless."

But a friend made a vow on Sukuru's behalf, and he was healed on Thaipusam Day. Sukuru took the name of the patron god Subramaniam. He is a painting contractor in Penang now fifty-two years old; he has three adult sons. And every year since 1946, he and his family have made their penance, a vow he will continue until his death.

On the final day of Thaipusam, the idol of Subramaniam returns to its former temple and George Town returns to its normal secular pursuits.

There is no easy explanation of the idolatrous mystery that is Thaipusam; moreover, it appears to demolish Jeremiah's contemptuous dismissal of an idol's powers. Certain critics of Christianity—Theodore Roszak among them—might leap at examples such as Thaipusam, assuming that the argument of Scripture against idolatry rests exclusively upon cultural snobbery. This rejection of idols, writes Roszak in *Where the Wasteland Ends*, results from an inability to recognize "the capacity of an icon or natural object to be enchanted." Here, it seems to me, Roszak is wrongheaded in his reasoning, for Jeremiah's description of idolatry doesn't explain wholly the Jewish and later the Christian case against worshiping manufactured or natural representations of deity.

Far from discounting occult powers, the man who mediated the Law of God against idolatry had also experienced those powers personally, for both good and evil: the bush burned but not consumed, the rod that became a serpent, the healthy hand that became leprous, then whole again; then feats accomplished by the pharaoh's magicians and necromancers. It wasn't cultural arrogance that caused Moses to order the destruction of the Golden Calf; it was his assurance, based upon what he knew and could see, that the manufactured idol had already been invested with powers to detract from the worship of Jehovah. Moses destroyed the idol, not because it was an impotent fraud, but because it was possessed by powers in opposition to the Word of God inscribed on the tablets. Moses destroyed the idol because the same power that gave Egyptian sorcerers their skill to convince the pharaoh had also degraded the Israelites and turned them into beasts.

Throughout the Old and New Testament, idolatry is regarded as foolish superstition; but it is also shown to be blasphemous, an abomination carrying with it deepest consequences. Throughout the history of the kings of Israel and Judah, the record measures a king's stature in relation to his idolatry or his faithfulness to the Lord God:

> But Omri did evil in the eyes of the LORD and sinned more than all those before him. He walked in all the ways of Jeroboam son of Nebat and in his sin, which he had caused Israel to commit, so that they provoked the LORD, the God of Israel, to anger by their worthless idols. . . .
>
> Ahab son of Omri became king of Israel. . . . [He] did more evil in the eyes of the LORD than any of those before him. He not only considered it trivial to commit the sins of Jeroboam son of Nebat, but he also married Jezebel daughter of Ethbaal king of the Sidonians, and began to serve Baal and worship him. He set up an altar for Baal in the temple of Baal that he built in Samaria. Ahab also made an Asherah pole and did more to provoke the LORD, the God of Israel, to anger than did all the kings of Israel before him (1 Kings 16:25-26, 30-33).
>
> Amaziah son of Joash king of Judah began to reign. He was twenty-five years old when he became king. . . . He did what was right in the eyes of the LORD, but not as his father David had done. In everything he followed the example of his father Joash. The high places, however, were not removed; the people continued to offer sacrifices and burn incense there (2 Kings 14:1-4).
>
> Hezekiah son of Ahaz king of Judah began to reign. . . . He did what was right in the eyes of the LORD, just as his father David had done. He removed the high places, smashed the sacred stones and cut down the Asherah poles. He broke into pieces the bronze snake Moses had made, for up to that time the Israelites had been burning incense to it. (It was called Nehushtan.)

Hezekiah trusted in the LORD, the God of Israel.
There was no one like him among all the kings of
Judah, either before him or after him (2 Kings 18:1,
3-6).

It's interesting to notice that Hezekiah refused to spare
even that historical monument, the Brazen Serpent, which had
been with the Israelites since their wilderness wanderings.
Perhaps Hezekiah was excessive in his iconoclasm; perhaps it
would have been sufficient merely to decree an end to all sac-
rifices before the ancient relic, now a thousand years old. But
Hezekiah wished to be thorough, to extirpate every evidence of
idolatry.

What motivated Hezekiah? Total obedience to the First
Commandment and concern over possible violation of the Second. So too in the early Christian church, one of the true marks
of a believer was his forsaking of idolatry. Paul urged his converts to avoid even the slightest appearance of respect for idols
by abstaining from eating meat offered in sacrifice, then sold to
profit the pagan priests.

The same principle holds today among Christians in countries where idolatrous sacrifice is common. In Japan and
Taiwan, in Bangladesh and India, I have observed Christians
by-passing one particular fruit seller or butcher because his
tangerines and bananas or his cuts of meat had been purchased
from the Buddhist temple or Hindu shrine.

THE POWER OF NEOPAGANISM

The idolatry of which we've been speaking so far is literal,
the kind that most appeals to a Western caricature—fashioning
images in the shape of man, beast, or demon. But idolatry may
also be figurative and lose none of its passion. Whatever fixation
holds a man in awe becomes his idolatrous god because it represents, in Paul Tillich's definition, "the elevation of a preliminary concern to ultimacy."

At an almost facetious level, our society has returned to

the primitive custom of deifying the weather. In spite of sophisticated meteorological satellites, weather forecasting technology, and suave television weather prophets, the popular mind has accepted designations of climatic disturbances by male and female names—"Albert," "Barbara," "Carol." Do we actually believe that we can lessen a natural phenomenon's potential for disaster by reducing it to human proportions? Ironically, in such personification a hurricane becomes mythologized into the fury and unpredictability of a monster.

Our society promulgates legends of the uncapturable phantom, the mysterious if not demonic beast. From biblical literature we learned of the monsters Leviathan and Rahab, denizens of primordial seas who could be tracked and trammeled only by God. The symbolism persists to this day, from Melville's Great White Whale to William Faulkner's bear or Hemingway's giant marlin. Those expeditions in search of the Himalayan yeti, the Loch Ness monster, the Big Foot or sasquatch of North American lore must be another case in point.

Of course, today's hunter in Western culture is seldom insuring his own survival; he's a sportsman or a conservationist. But, in fact, deer hunting in the Catskills or big-game fishing in the Caribbean is more than outdoor recreation. It's the continuation of a primeval tradition, with a prize as the subject of ritual. Obligatory photographs of the hunter with his kill, or the preservation through taxidermy of a set of antlers or a marlin's head to display above the mantelpiece: these are, in their own ways, the making of idols. Is it even too much to suggest that distributing copies of the photograph or inviting other members of the hunting party to see the stuffed trophy is part of the sacred ritual? For it recalls a sacred moment in our secular world—a moment when man and beast were engaged together in testimony to the consecration of life and the sanctification of death. Indeed, did not the beast's death bring dignity to the man's life?

Wherever secularism dominates, idolatry extends beyond paganism to symbols of power, to the adoration of celebrities both popular and political. Augustus, Louis XIV, and other absolute monarchs in their day regarded themselves as deserving of worship; today's popular deities—athletes, movie actors and actresses, musicians, other entertainers—seek no less the fawning adulation of the masses. We have moved from an idolatry of class to an idolatry of charisma, measured by a performer's sex appeal and the manner in which personal appearance influences the all-important ratings.

For it is perfectly obvious that popular idolatry has been spawned by the modern media. A burgeoning technology has made possible the overnight apotheosis of a pretty face. Through the photo magazine, motion pictures, radio, recordings, and television, an unknown country boy can be "hyped" into the center of a worldwide cult. The Beatles may be the best example of this phenomenon. Starting out in Liverpool in the late fifties, they were a ragtag group of ruffians, hardly distinguishable from other "Teddy Boys" of the time. Yet after their 1964 introduction to America on "The Ed Sullivan Show," the Beatles emerged as objects of worship by their fanatics. So great was their popularity that it isn't at all farfetched to say, with Jeff Greenfield, "They changed rock, which changed the culture, which changed us."

Such is the power of the modern media, especially television. It can whet popular fanaticism until the public bows in obeisance before any idol the technocrats select. Opinion polls actively determine attitudes, rather than passively recording them. News broadcasts follow the same course, determining by what is left unsaid and cut from film the slant of today's news. We recognize overt commercial advertising by its high decibels; we sometimes note the subtle introduction of products into viewing prominence. But none of us, at ease in our family rooms before our twenty-five-inch color set, can hope to know how frequently we are being bombarded by subliminal messages, like microdots; nor do we know the force these messages have upon our subconscious levels of perception and decision. George Orwell's novel *1984* predicted the power of the screen to control a society through propaganda, but it's doubtful that even Orwell would have believed his vision to be so nearly correct.

In many parts of the world, the idol takes the shape of the totalitarian State and its titular head, whose disembodied form is known only by huge photograph and televised image. To anyone who knows history, the power of a demagogue to deceive is always a mystery. But we have no cause to linger long berating those who give their religious fervor in idolatry to the State. They may be what Marullus in *Julius Caesar* calls the common people of Rome, "You blocks, you stones, you worse than senseless things!" But they are hardly any more thickheaded or deluded in political idolatry than many Americans, for whom the Stars 'n' Stripes is no mere flag but a fetish.

Arnold Toynbee points out that nationalist idolatry is an inheritance from the Greeks, a concomitant of the fifteenth and sixteenth centuries' renaissance of Greek culture:

> The Greek attitude towards the local city-states of the Greek World was one of worship. These states were the true gods of the Ancient Greek World, and the Greeks were conscious of what they were doing and frank in acknowledging it. They consciously symbolized their worship of their city-states by presenting these in the form of goddesses.

During the rebirth of Hellenism in Western Europe, Toynbee continues,

> this Greek idolatrous attitude towards one's own country, one's own fatherland, was imported from the Ancient Greek past back into our modern Western life.

But, Toynbee insists, there is a grave difference between the two forms of nationalism:

> Unlike the Greeks, we have flinched from openly admitting that we are practicing this form of idolatry; and, consequently, we are even more at the mercy of this idolatrous type of Nationalism than the Greeks were at the mercy of their more frankly avowed idolatrous worship of their local states.

What does Toynbee mean? Of course there is much to admire in patriotism, much to honor in the courage and fortitude of those who have sacrificed their lives so that succeeding generations might live free. But this noble virtue is a private one, as all virtues must be. It becomes corrupted as soon as it becomes institutionalized. A simple swelling of homeland pride within an individual becomes the screaming obscenity of the Nazis' *"Sieg Heil"* at Nuremberg.

Not all Germans were Nazis. Nor is the American super-patriot so easy to identify. Conventionally, he is supposed to be a Southern redneck, all but illiterate, violent in his prejudices, a sentimentalist who weeps when he hears the band strike up, "O say, can you see." But such regionalism is unfair. What Aldous Huxley called "the religion of idolatrous nationalism" is as prevalent among New York City's policemen or Southern California's junior executives as it may be among Maine lobstermen or Mississippi Delta cotton farmers. Archie Bunker makes his home all over America.

The nature of civil idolatry, however, is somewhat more difficult to explain. An essay by Robert N. Bellah, "Civil Religion in America," describes the phenomenon. In spite of Constitutional restriction against establishing any religion, American civil religion is established and maintained, Bellah says, through public ceremonies such as the inauguration of a President, Memorial Day obsequies, the annual proclamation of Thanksgiving Day; and, he adds, "the public-school system serves as a particularly important context for the cultic celebration of the civil rituals." Oversimplified, grossly generalized by teachers whose understanding of history is seldom from primary sources, the study of American history collapses into platitudes. In *The King and I*, the young prince rejects as false a map that shows Siam as a tiny country among the nations of the world. He had been taught to believe otherwise! So American school-children grow up to accept as true only those elements of American history we wish them to learn. Their ignorance becomes the basis for perpetuating our civil religion.

Civil religion is highly moralistic. It also relies upon cant and jingoism, with heavy emphasis upon generalization and the bandwagon appeal. Civil religion is a bumper-sticker dogma that lends itself more readily to slogans than to thought. "America: Love it or leave it!" is a favorite expression of rearguard patriotism. More often than not, the litany of civil religion includes a pairing of exhortations such as "Honor America" and "Stop Busing." Civil religion also assumes an inherent right to determine what does or does not constitute loyalty.

The American novelist James Baldwin has written, "I love America more than any other country in the world, and exactly for this reason, I insist on the right to criticize her perpetually." But to many who glory in their love of country, Baldwin's statement is incongruous, if not disloyal. They can't understand why anyone would want to change any facet of American life. They view suspiciously any form of government not identical to American democracy; if possible, they support efforts to compel democracy upon weaker nations. They see only through rosy spectacles. For them, America is like "Home on the Range"—

> Where never is heard a discouraging word,
> And the skies are not cloudy all day.

Civil religion presumes a bond between love of country and love for God—"America the Beautiful" and "God Said It. I Believe It. That Settles It." Such ardor might concur with Scripture, if American patriots were willing to allow citizens of other countries to express the same love for their homelands. All too often, American loyalty declines into sheer chauvinism—what Arnold Toynbee called "the worship of the collective power of Man in place of the worship of God." The result is a refusal to step beyond an uncritical recitation of all the things that "make America great." The attitude is well expressed in the fourth stanza of the National Anthem:

> Then conquer we must, when our cause it is just,
> And this be our motto, "In God is our trust."

Chauvinism to this degree is often compounded by a faulty interpretation of an alleged Christian heritage from our American forefathers. Bellah points out that, while American civil religion is "neither sectarian nor in any specific sense Christian," still the Christian presuppositions hover somewhere overhead. Yet the principal tenet of the American political idolatry is "faith in faith." President Dwight D. Eisenhower is reported to have gushed, "Our government makes no sense unless it is founded in a deeply felt religious faith—and I don't care what that faith is." Such platitudes suit well the vapid rhetoric of American civil religion. To suggest any set of beliefs more categorical than Eisenhower's is to risk becoming doctrinaire. All that's required is fatuous recitation of slogans proclaiming loyalty to our most popular traditions.

Even corporations from time to time remind us of the American Gospel. In *The Wall Street Journal*, Tiffany and Company displays an advertisement asking, "Is Inflation The Real Problem?"

> No, it is not. Inflation is simply the inevitable final result of our follies. What, then, are the real causes of this national calamity?

Boldly the Tiffany ad declares its opinion—exorbitant and unwise government spending, bureaucratic regulations, crippling taxes, excessive generosity to foreign countries, waste in war. Then Tiffany lays its final charge for today's economic woes:

> Forsaking our religious heritage, not only in our schools, but everywhere, thus accentuating crime, immorality, greed and selfishness.

But what about "our religious heritage"? Overlooking the material concerns that motivated the Pilgrim Fathers at least as much as their far-fabled quest for religious freedom—overlooking the barbarity and intolerance of the Puritan theocracy—we come upon an anomaly in American civil religion. This is the virtual canonization of men as American saints whose own written testimony bears little relationship to orthodox Christian doctrine. For example, Thomas Paine rejected the Bible as "hearsay," preferring to believe that "the word of God is the creation we behold." Thomas Jefferson also disparaged the Bible, citing "reason" as "the only oracle given you by heaven." Jefferson's inclusive faith warned him against questioning "the different roads we may pursue, as believing them the shortest, to that our last abode." He held, instead, that

> following the guidance of a good conscience, let us
> be happy in the hope that by these different paths we
> shall all meet in the end.

Here, of course, is natural religion, the creedless creed of American democracy.

Benjamin Franklin was even more explicit in his denial of New Testament doctrine. In a letter to Ezra Stiles, president of Yale College, written shortly before his death, the wit of *Poor Richard's Almanac* overtook Franklin:

> As to Jesus of Nazareth, . . . I have some doubts as
> to his divinity; though it is a question I do not dog-
> matize upon, having never studied it, and think it
> needless to busy myself with it now, when I expect
> soon an opportunity of knowing the truth with less
> trouble.

Both Franklin and Jefferson were also cautious about expressing even so skeletal a framework of faith as this. "Our particular principles of religion are a subject of accountability to our God alone," wrote Jefferson. "I inquire after no man's, and trouble none with mine." So today, a maxim of American etiquette is, "Never discuss politics or religion." Above all, one must avoid allowing any private religious beliefs to affect public behavior. This was the promise made by John F. Kennedy to Protestant ministers in Houston during the 1960 election campaign: He would be an American first, a Roman Catholic second. A generation later, during the 1984 presidential campaign, the Roman Catholic hierarchy found itself at odds with several prominent American politicians, including the first woman candidate for vice-president, Geraldine Ferraro, and New York State's governor, Mario Cuomo, over the same issues. What some candidates and elected officials called "the wall of separation between church and state" their critics recognized as political expediency.

Civil religion is at war with Christianity, although some Christians haven't yet heard the news. A declaration of that irreconcilable struggle was given by Jesus himself in a subtle reply frequently misunderstood: "Then give to Caesar what is Caesar's, and to God what is God's" (Luke 20:25). Since only appearances belong to any temporal power and all that is real belongs to God alone, can there be any doubt of what Jesus meant? Yet even earnest Christians can be trapped into identifying patriotism with obedience to God. "We are always relapsing," wrote Toynbee,

> from the worship of God into the worship of our tribe or of ourselves, and therefore we Christians . . . tend to treat Christianity as if it were the tribal religion of our particular civilization. In the West, we tend to treat it as something that derives its virtue not so much from being Christian as from being Western.

We need to be summoned out of apathy towards self-righteous arrogance and pernicious idolatry that reduce God to a national mascot. The clarion may have been sounded in a brief speech given by Senator Mark O. Hatfield of Oregon. On 1 February 1973, at the annual National Prayer Breakfast, Senator Hatfield broke through the smugness of the occasion, addressing an audience which included then president Richard M. Nixon, his vice-president Spiro T. Agnew, Supreme Court justices, cabinet members, and congressmen. He said, in part,

> As we gather at this prayer breakfast, let us beware of the real danger of misplaced allegiance, if not outright idolatry, to the extent we fail to distinguish

between the god of an American civil religion and the God who reveals himself in the Holy Scriptures and in Jesus Christ.

If we as leaders appeal to the god of civil religion, our faith is in a small and exclusive deity, a loyal spiritual Advisor to power and prestige, a Defender of only the American nation, the object of a national folk religion devoid of moral content. But if we pray to the Biblical God of justice and righteousness, we fall under God's judgment for calling upon his name, but failing to obey his commands.

We need to be reminded that, as Senator Hatfield says, civil religion robs genuine faith of its integrity; it dulls the cutting edge of prophetic criticism. "Thus saith the Lord . . ." becomes "With all due respect. . . ." Throughout the period of the Nixon-Agnew perfidy, did established worship services in the East Room of the White House ever hear a Micaiah willing to declare, "As surely as the LORD lives, I can tell him only what the LORD tells me"? Or a Simon Peter telling the authorities, "We must obey God rather than men!'"? Instead of driving out of the temple those who traded in corruption, political sabotage, and deceit, timid prophets of civil religion took seats next to the offenders. The result became an unhealthy union of Americanism with mere religiosity—a politicized amalgam of the Judeo-Christian ethic robbed of its spiritual dynamic, secularized beyond recognition. Now, with the disclosures of hypocrisy in high places, a coating of cynicism has tarred public profession of Christian faith, as each presidential campaign since 1976 has disclosed.

Civil religion is *no* religion; it's a demagogic fraud. A Christian in America, if he is true to the teachings of Jesus Christ, should not expect to be in the majority; in fact, he'll almost always be unpopular to those in positions of authority. Not because he sets out to be obnoxious personally, but because the character of his life testifies against everything secular the power brokers represent. Compromisers—those who have bowed the knee to the baals of civil religion—must hear again the sermon of Father Mapple in *Moby-Dick*:

> Woe to him whom this world charms from Gospel duty! Woe to him who seeks to pour oil upon the waters when God has brewed them into a gale! Woe to him who seeks to please rather than to appal! Woe to him whose good name is more to him than goodness! Woe to him who, in this world, courts not dishonor! Woe to him who would not be true, even though to be false were salvation!

A generation ago, Toynbee warned against the co-opting of Christianity by civil religion. He spoke of "the spectacle of the local national flag—a symbol of the idolatrous worship of some local state—being carried into a Christian church, and sometimes . . . the Cross and a national flag being carried in church in the same procession." In America, of course, the so-called "Christian Flag" often stands opposite the Stars 'n' Stripes. "Whenever I see that," Toynbee continues,

> I find myself filled with foreboding. Here are two rival religions: traditional Christianity and neo-paganism. . . . In the inevitable future war to the death between them, which of them is going to win? Here are their symbols, side by side, being borne aloft, with an apparently equal veneration, within the walls of the same consecrated building. For how long can they continue to co-exist?

What will it take before Americans realize the futility of political idolatry? What more must happen to bring down in pieces the great god Dagon in our Philistine temple? Haven't we already lived through more than enough national tragedy to convince us, once and for all, that God isn't an American and that the colors of Heaven aren't red, white, and blue?

Unpatriotic? Of course not! The true citizen of any nation knows the promise suggested by Melville's preacher:

"Delight,—top-gallant delight is to him who acknowledges no law or lord, but the Lord his God, and is only a patriot to heaven."

THE WORSHIP OF MAN

In every age, in every culture, the human race turns in awe to worship scarecrows in its own melon patch—idols in whom to invest powers that speak somehow of a reality beyond ourselves. But in the Secular Age, a new idol has been raised; or rather, the oldest idol has been re-enshrined. The object of gratification in Eden was not the forbidden fruit but equality with God; Abel's murder signified Cain's rejection of God's justice; at Babel, the full fury of mankind's rebellion against God's supreme authority asserted itself in egocentricity.

Ultimate idolatry is the worship of man himself. In the scholarship of comparative religion, it isn't a great distance between the most primitive icons and the development of idols in human form. In religious chronology, god-made-in-the-image-of-man is a relatively early phase. Every other act of idolatry leads to this climax, and true atheism grows not from any denial that God exists but from the declaration, "I myself am God!" From this self-affirmation—this rebellion against any innate sensibility toward higher authority—may be traced the decadence into a search for autonomous, anarchistic man. Out of this search grow societies without need for redeeming values or sanctifying graces; families without respect for ancestry or posterity; individuals without concern for anyone other than themselves.

Today's Secular Man has acquired a sophistication to accompany his self-esteem, a creed by which to affirm his own venerable worth. It's a slogan which John Baillie claims gave birth to "the egocentric predicament"; a catch-word coined at the moment which William Temple, late Archbishop of Canterbury, calls "perhaps the most disastrous in the history of Europe." What is this provocative phrase? Rene Descartes's *Cogito, ergo sum*: "I think, therefore I am."

The effect of Descartes's declaration was to reduce man from a spiritual to a rational being. "I think," said the philosopher. Why not, "I love"? Why not, "I serve"? Why not, "I give"? By limiting his ontological evidence to thinking, Descartes did away with qualitative arguments for human existence, neutralizing human experience into a mechanical paradigm of impulse/reaction. As Jacques Maritain points out in *The Dream of Descartes*, the French mathematician wasn't interested in *what* he thinks or *why*. This is because the ultimate end of Cartesian reasoning is not really to know but "to subjugate the object." Thus, Maritain writes,

> Cartesian evidence goes straight to mechanism. It mechanizes nature, it does violence to it; it annihilates everything which causes things to symbolize with the spirit, to partake of the genius of the Creator, to speak to us. The universe becomes dumb.

And so, Maritain laments, "Rationalism is the death of spirituality."

What, then, are the consequences of Cartesian egocentricity and the split between things of the spirit and mere "thinking"? In Maritain's view, the consequences are a rejection of the spiritual for the corporeal, the metaphysical for the mechanical, the moral for the technological. And it all began, says Maritain, by "putting the human self above everything else, an angelic self—nay, a divine self."

Now, perhaps, we can perceive that, whereas we thought idolatry was a wheel turning away from secularism, the two have found a nexus. The essence of secularity is at its meshing with idolatry, precisely at the point of man's adoration of himself. "Here is man then," says Maritain in derision, "the center of the world." On the one hand, secularly denying the existence of any reality beyond empirical proof; and on the other, idolatrously designing a religion with himself as the sole object of worship.

Chapter 4

The Secret at the Center: A Christian Cosmology

When I was ten years old, I began to develop my passion for sport, baseball in particular. My beloved Detroit Tigers were on their way to winning the American League pennant, perhaps the World Series. For my own part, I was no athlete. In fact, my mother was so embarrassed at my inability to catch a ball, she made me join her outside the parsonage each evening after supper. There she'd select one of the scores of wormy apples that had fallen; then setting me a few paces away from her, she'd throw to me until I'd caught the apple ten times without dropping it. After each success, I'd take another pace backwards.

Of course, there was no television in those days, and we lived too far from Briggs Stadium ever to attend a game. My contact with the Tigers—and I knew every one of them, from Manager Steve O'Neill to his son-in-law shortstop, Spider Webb—was Harry Heilmann, the play-by-play announcer on the radio broadcasts of each game. Somehow, in those days of strictest legalism, I was permitted to listen, except on Sundays, even though the broadcasts were sponsored by Goebel's beer.

That summer of 1945 is also memorable for me because

our family made one of our first extended trips. We visited New York City for the first time, and there a strange eagerness came over me. In a city then boasting not one but three professional baseball teams, including the hated Yankees—mortal enemies of "Prince Hal" Newhouser, Paul Richards, Hank Greenberg, and the rest of my heroes—I had no wish to see any baseball game. I wanted to see the Hayden Planetarium.

I'd found a book in our Michigan village library—my mother was also the librarian—called *The Sky Above Us*, published by the American Museum of Natural History and its Planetarium. The book had so fascinated me with its pictures of telescopes, meteors, nebulae, and the rest of astronomical lore, I was ready to forsake my life's ambition to become a sportscaster and take up astronomy. I became a star gazer. I took to walking with my neck arched, my head wrenched backward, so that I could better observe the constellations. A log recorded every shooting star I saw.

When the opportunity came to sightsee in New York City, I chose the Planetarium as my special treat. It didn't disappoint me then; it never has since. What I remember best, however, is the model of the solar system in the waiting room just outside the sky-show auditorium. This model, based on the Copernican theory of a heliocentric universe, gave me my first awareness of immensity. It was also my first introduction to cosmology.

Explaining the universe as an ordered entity is the purpose of any cosmology; to do so, cosmology must depend upon models. Among the most familiar is an ancient Indian model: the planet Earth is like a brass tea tray resting on the backs of three elephants who, in turn, stand upon the shell of a tortoise. In the Middle East, under Babylonian mythology, a three-tiered universe became the accepted model: the firmament above, the earth surrounded by water, an empty region of the dead beneath. To most school-children, the clockwork model or orrery in the Planetarium, based upon a 1715 invention by George Graham and named for his patron, the Fourth Earl of Orrery, is the impression they hold for life. It becomes our cosmology, our explanation of how the solar system functions, and satisfies by its simplicity our need to know our place in that system.

Yet today, far more sophisticated cosmologies exist to show us that the universe has no known or knowable physical center. Its vastness can be spoken of only in terms of infinitude. "The sun is but a morning star," wrote Henry D. Thoreau in *Walden*, perhaps more wisely than he knew, for far from being the center of the universe, the sun can scarcely claim to be more than a minor light in its own galaxy.

This loss of the center has destabilized mankind in more ways than the astronomical. Almost every cosmology before our own modern nebular explanation of the universe revered a sacred place within its system where the gods—who usually dwell elsewhere—are said to grant men a transcendent revelation of themselves. Often such a place becomes known as "the center of the earth," "the axis of the world," and so on. The idea of the Center is, as Mircea Eliade says, "preeminently the zone of the sacred, the zone of absolute reality." Because its precincts are holy, an altar may be built, a temple erected, a sacred pillar raised to symbolize the *axis mundi*. Sometimes the presence of a high mountain gives the location its own divine aura. The Oglala Sioux holy man Black Elk tells of his momentous vision in these terms:

> I looked ahead and saw the mountains there with rocks and forests on them, and from the mountains flashed all colors upward to the heavens. Then I was standing on the highest mountain of them all, and round about beneath me was the whole hoop of the world. And while I stood there I saw more than I can tell and I understood more than I saw; for I was seeing in a sacred manner the shapes of all things in the spirit, and the shapes of all shapes as they must live together like one being. And I saw that the sacred hoop of my people was one of many hoops that made one circle, wide as daylight and as starlight, and in the center grew one mighty flowering tree to shelter

all the children of one mother and one father. And I
saw that it was holy.

Nearly one hundred miles northwest of Athens, in Greece,
lies Delphi, the most sacred shrine of classical antiquity. Set in
a natural bowl under looming cliffs of Mount Parnassus, Delphi
was known to the Greeks as the *omphalos*, the very navel of the
earth. Sacred to several deities, it was renowned throughout the
Mediterranean world as the seat of Apollo's oracle. According
to one legend devotees of Apollo may in fact have been responsible for construction of similar shrines as far away as
Stonehenge in England. Many mysteries and rites now lost to
time may have been enacted at Delphi. The Castalian spring,
for example, flowing from Parnassus through the gorge of the
Phaedriades, or "Shining Rocks," was said to be the source of
poetic inspiration; in time, the inspiring Muses themselves were
thought to have found their permanent home on Parnassus at
Delphi.

But it was as Apollo's shrine that Delphi was best known,
for here the most human of the Greek gods had overcome the
great serpent Python and wrested from Gaea, goddess of the
Earth, control of its center. Here too he established his oracle,
famous for her equivocal responses and dire predictions.

Worship of Apollo at Delphi may have begun more than
thirty-five hundred years ago, but its traditions were certainly
well established by the beginning of the sixth century B.C. By
then, the primacy of Delphi among sacred shrines was also
clearly accepted. Pilgrims were coming from throughout the
Greek world, bringing with them their treasures, intending to
enter into the veneration of the god through sacrifice and expiation, hoping to carry with them some word of guidance and hope
for the future.

The pilgrim's rites at Delphi began at the Castalian spring,
with purification in its icy waters. From there, the pilgrim en-
tered the Sacred Precinct and ascended the Sacred Way, past
monuments to votive performance of the same ritual by previous worshipers. On his way, he would purchase an animal for

sacrifice—perhaps, as Keats imagined, "that heifer lowing at the skies,/And all her silken flanks with garlands dressed." Together with other pilgrims he would climb toward Apollo's temple.

Along the route he would pass through long porticos in which were displayed statues to mark various victories attributed to Apollo's intervention: for instance, the naval battle at Salamis, in 480 B.C., when the Greeks had defeated the Persian fleet. Each city-state also had its own treasury, a small marble structure resembling a temple, in which were collected offerings of the faithful from Athens, Thebes, and other locales. The pilgrim passing by was expected to leave his token of gratitude— a coin, a piece of jewelry—his offering to Apollo.

All along the Sacred Way, the procession encountered musicians playing and singing their paeans to Apollo, god of music as well as of physical beauty.

At the next bend of the narrow track, the pilgrim came to the Temple itself. The present ruins, built on the site of five earlier structures, date from 330 B.C. Several of its Doric columns still rise sixty feet tall, suggesting the original building's spaciousness. A ramp, cross-grooved for the hooves of the sacrificial animals, leads to where the great altar once stood. Beyond it, the pilgrim would have seen the priestess sitting on a tripod stool at a point in the floor of the temple where intoxicating vapors emanated from the mountain's slopes. After making his sacrifice, the pilgrim might consult the oracle, hoping not to hear again her most fearful saying: "Your son shall kill his father and marry his mother."

There were no written scriptures for this cult at Delphi. Its propagation depended upon dramatic productions in the theatre, reenacting significant events in the myth of Apollo. There the pilgrim heard and saw again stories that confirmed his faith. In the theatre at Delphi, as in Athens's Theatre of Dionysus, playwrights were required to depict events already familiar to their audiences; the dramatist's imagination in reconstructing the myth was the measure of his art. His play, however, was no mere entertainment. It was, as Bernard Grebanier notes, "the religious equivalent of the Hebraic-Christian practice of fasting on the Day of Atonement or during Lent." On the stage below the sweeping Delphic amphitheater, worshipers witnessed in awe the wonder-workings of the god they had come to Delphi to honor.

But these rites continued beyond confirmation through drama to personal dedication of the body in athletic fitness and sometimes in competition. Returning down the Sacred Way and past the Castalian spring, the pilgrim came upon the gymnasium and *palestra*, or wrestling chamber, with its hot mineral baths. Here the departing pilgrim might pause for a final act of exercise in worship of the most athletic of the gods. And every four years, at intervals midway through the observance of each Olympiad, the stadium at Delphi hosted the Pythian Games, to observe the victory of Apollo over the dread serpent Python.

These games, like those at Olympia, antedate history, but we know that they were reinstituted in 582 B.C., and continued until 393 A.D., when the Roman emperor Theodosius ended the rites at Delphi and elsewhere throughout Greece. The Pythian Games consisted of foot races, wrestling and boxing matches, the five events called pentathlon, and horse-and-chariot races, although because of Parnassus's steepness, these latter spectacles had to be held in the valley below. Uniquely at Delphi, the Pythian Games also included competition in musicianship, held probably in the theatre.

The horseshoe stadium had great pedestals at its open end, presumably to house statues of Apollo. In the exact middle of the stadium, a special bench was set aside for the judges. Before them came each victor to receive his prize—a simple wreath of laurel leaves taken from the tree sacred to the god.

All these timeless ceremonies, however idolatrous, adumbrate much that remains in the ritual of modern religion: the journey away from ordinary concerns to a sacred place; there, purification and sacrifice, offering and expiation, exhortation through prophecy or attestation to divine powers in dramatic reenactment; finally, the dedication of soul and body to service.

Fittingly, these rites, whether at Delphi or at the little church around the corner, must be conducted at "the Center of the Earth"—at some point consecrated for worship. For it is at the Center that humanity seeks most earnestly for a relationship with the divine. Even when removed from this most sacred shrine, a religious person has learned that one may participate in the sanctity of the Center. For wherever, like Jacob, he acknowledges that "the Lord is in this place," there he may also go on to say, "This is none other than the house of God; this is the gate of heaven" (Genesis 28:16-17).

At such a place a religious man may build his most personal shrine, that is, his own house. The sacred sign given to assure him of his relationship to the gods has been given at that place. It becomes, therefore, his most fitting temporal home, symbolic of the true and higher home where dwell the gods. Similarly the erection of public buildings, housing officers of government to conduct affairs of state, represents the vision of an ordered universe governed by the Judge of All the World. It is perfectly understandable that men should enshrine within the very center of such a building's cornerstone their most precious documents.

Yet, even while the faithful journeyed to Delphi, a fifth-century-B.C. philosopher, the Sophist Protagoras, gave intellectual respectability, first to agnosticism and then to the establishing of a new center—a revision of the fixed point. His treatise *On the Gods* begins:

> About the gods, I have no means of knowing whether they exist or do not exist or what their form may be. Many things prevent the attainment of this knowledge, the obscurity of the subject and the fact that man's life is short.

Ironically, this fragment is all that remains of Protagoras's religious skepticism. But its consequences are evident and ongoing in his work *On Truth*, which begins with this fateful declaration: "Man is the measure of all things."

Secular Man is the disciple of Protagoras. He claims for

himself the center ring in the circus of life. A bumper sticker I once saw on the Long Island Expressway sums up this egocentricity: "Man Is God." The practical results of such boasting are nothing short of man's declared supremacy in the cosmos: Secular Man is lord of the universe.

But what kind of impostor is this pretender to cosmic lordship? Yeats describes Secular Man's kingdom in the apocalyptic poem, "The Second Coming":

> Turning and turning in the widening gyre
> The falcon cannot hear the falconer;
> Things fall apart; the centre cannot hold;
> Mere anarchy is loosed upon the world,
> The blood-dimmed tide is loosed, and everywhere
> The ceremony of innocence is drowned;
> The best lack all conviction, while the worst
> Are full of passionate intensity.

Perhaps Black Elk, reflecting upon the aftermath of broken treaties by a faithless secular government and material greed by a secularized society, is right in characterizing the imprisonment of his people in these words: "There is no center any longer, and the sacred tree is dead."

A Place to Stand

Where you find the Center depends largely upon your cosmology or model for the universe—what German philosophers and theologians call *Weltanschauung*, the world-and-life view, the individual's "angle of vision." This metaphor of stance, posture, platform, attitude, or observation suggests that every thinking man or woman has chosen a place to stand and see the world. From that vantage point, everything else takes its shape, everything falls into perspective.

One person may take her world-and-life view from an emergency ward: the entire world, as it were, in tourniquet and splint. Another sees his world from the bottom of a garbage can: the world as trash. Still another may view the world through rose-colored glasses: the world as a summer idyll. Prince Hamlet offers his view as of "an unweeded garden/That grows to seed; things rank and gross in nature/ Possess it merely." From whatever view of life one holds, character is molded until an inherent relationship grows between life principles and action. Adherents to every ideology eventually come to understand that the position they take and the view of life they assume both informs their intellect and affects their behavior.

In the political sphere, this relationship between belief and action can be illustrated by the story of a foreign traveler's experience on board a jetliner in the People's Republic of China during the Cultural Revolution. The foreigner noticed that the Chinese stewardess, instead of offering coffee, tea, or martini, was speaking to herself—reciting, he was told, the sayings of Chairman Mao Zedong. When asked why, she replied, "The sayings of Chairman Mao keep the plane aloft."

This young woman had found a place to stand and see the world. To dramatize the metaphor further, she had taken her stand in the mouth of a cave in the mountains of northwest China, at the end of the Long March. From that vantage she had looked out and seen the glorious potential of a workers' paradise. The Soviet Marxist, somewhat more abstractly, finds himself within the whirling vortex of the movement of history, from thesis to antithesis to synthesis and beyond. Inside this dialectical maelstrom, the Marxist looks out to see a proletarian revolution and the State supreme.

However much one may disagree with the Maoist or Marxist visions they have, at least, the apparent quality of purposefulness. They are apocalyptic, looking optimistically for better times to come. By contrast, the secular world-and-life view, with nothing greater than puny man to glorify, offers poor fare indeed. It's at best a Barmecide feast, a fantasy of abundance denying the reality of spiritual famine. Secular Man claims to be at the center of all existence; yet the very nature of his careening course argues against him. Centrifugal forces drive him to the outer rim of despair and suicide, while centripetal powers of reason compel him back to seek his true Center.

While Secular Man spins dervish-like in search of this fixed point in the universe, still another view insists on being recognized. This is the Christian world-and-life view. The Christian takes his label from his belief that Jesus of Nazareth was the Christ, God's Messenger. Thus the Christian takes his stand where Jesus most transcendently revealed himself—at the foot of the Cross and at the door of the Empty Tomb. The Christian looks out and sees all he knows of life on this planet, its human and natural inhabitants. To him it isn't the whole world; only a grain of sand in the universe-at-large. The Christian regards the cosmos as having been lovingly created by a personal God wishing to make himself known to his creation. But the Christian believes that this fly-speck of creation, this planet Earth, became alienated from its Creator by sin and its consequences; however, the Christian also sees that God the Creator chose to reconcile this planet unto himself. The Christian sees that all of life may be redeemed and a new relationship with God made possible through the sacrifice of Jesus Christ on the cross and his resurrection power over death.

The warrant for the Christian world-and-life view must ultimately come from the authority of sacred Scripture. But even before accepting the testimony of the Bible, that "God was in Christ," other evidence may be offered. There is, first, an insatiable human yearning for a personal relationship between man and his Idea of the Holy. Scoffers attempting to debunk religion in general, Christianity in particular, sometimes refer to the human quest for a Father-figure as if this longing were proof of some aberration. Far from it! Is it considered strange that a foundling child reaches an age when he must seek to know who his parents were? Aren't there now agencies to assist adopted children in locating their natural fathers and mothers? Are these aberrant behaviors? Or do they confirm our natural urge to know and love and be loved by a father? And if so, doesn't this urge derive from some higher source and model?

Furthermore, myth and prophecy from every human tribe assure mankind of a coming hero-redeemer who will rescue us from the serpent Python, from the sea-monster Tiamat, from that old dragon Satan. Every society studied by cultural anthropologists knows this promise. Often the hero is supposed to have made his appearance at some time in the distant past; however, his coming is at best an evanescent memory from some transhistorical age, ritualized perhaps but without permanent efficacy. That memory has become, in reality, a dim foreshadowing of an event they still await.

But the Christian claim audaciously declares that the myth whose fulfillment the world awaits has indeed "become fact," as C. S. Lewis says. The hero by whom the languishing world expects deliverance is none other than Jesus of Nazareth. He is unique in history. At Christmas, we celebrate the miracle of a child born in Bethlehem's manger; but we also adore the mystery of the Word-Made-Flesh. Jesus was born, but the Eternal Word *became flesh*. The Logos, at whose command the cosmos was called into being, from eternal preexistence became human. This is the meaning of the Incarnation.

So Scripture declares, but so too history confirms, for the Incarnation is the pivotal event of history, the very Center of human experience. Before the Incarnation, human beings lived under what Mircea Eliade calls "the terror of history," seeking to console themselves either by abolishing history through annual rituals recreating the world as they knew it, or by accepting a cyclical theory of history through the myth of eternal repetition. Since the fact of Jesus' life, death, and resurrection, however, the human race has received a new vision of history: it is not a series of overlapping or concentric circles but continuous, linear history with a beginning and an end.

To overcome the terror of history means to find freedom in a universe enslaved by fear. But such freedom comes only by an act of faith in the One with power to set men free—the Liberating Word! The Word who first summoned the cosmos at its creation: the Word who will again call the cosmos to its final consummation at the end of time. Faith in Jesus of Nazareth recognizes his sovereignty as Lord of time and space. He is the Lord

Jesus, the Christ or Messenger of God.

We find this beautifully, succinctly expressed in the early church hymn quoted by Paul in his letter to the Colossians:

> He is the image of the invisible God, the firstborn over all creation. For by him all things were created: things in heaven and on earth, visible and invisible, whether thrones or powers or rulers or authorities; all things were created by him and for him. He is before all things, and in him all things hold together. And he is the head of the body, the church; he is the beginning and the firstborn from among the dead, so that in everything he might have the supremacy. For God was pleased to have all his fullness dwell in him, and through him to reconcile to himself all things, whether things on earth or things in heaven, by making peace through his blood, shed on the cross (Colossians 1:15-20).

The most striking feature of this passage is its uncompromising insistence upon the uniqueness of the Incarnate God. Its claims are all-encompassing, unremitting in their totality. Here is a categorical, unqualified declaration that Jesus is the physical embodiment of the Godhead; as such, he is worthy to be called Creator, Sustainer, Redeemer, and Reconciler. But these comprehensive assertions of power depend upon primary recognition of Jesus as "the image of the invisible God." This is the paradox over which many people stumble: How can there be a visible representation of invisible holiness?

The mystery resolves itself in these simple words: "For God *was pleased* to have all his fullness dwell in him." To believe in God means that one grants to deity the power of deity. If God is God, he must be permitted the right to express his will by whatever means he chooses. Strangely, many who balk at recognizing in the Person of Jesus the fullness of God are perfectly willing to see God in nature, in music, in a gesture of love. If there, why not see him supremely manifest in the One

Person whose claim has most validity? Especially when Scripture so declares.

This paean also reveals the purpose of the Incarnation. Why did God invest himself in a physical human body? Again, it was God's own choice, the divine means of reconciling to himself all things. Teilhard de Chardin, whose literalism scandalizes many readers used to making metaphorical rationalizations, sees the Incarnation as God's way of reunifying the cosmos, shattered into fragments by sin. "Christ's humanity was chosen," writes Père Teilhard, "to serve as the instrument of this unification in which the unravelled skein of all the fibres of the universe is woven into one." Teilhard believes in the physical corporeality of Jesus, but he also argues that

> through his Incarnation he entered not only into mankind but also into the universe that bears mankind—and this he did, not simply in the capacity of an element associated with it, but with the dignity and function of directive principle, of center upon which every form of love and every affinity converge. Mysterious and vast though the mystical Body already be, it does not, accordingly, exhaust the immense and bountiful integrity of the Word made flesh. Christ has a cosmic body that extends throughout the whole universe.

The Colossian hymn to the Incarnation goes on to make an equally shocking claim about the God-in-Flesh we call Jesus of Nazareth. This claim is wholly outrageous—unless it too is true. He is not only divine but, according to the New Testament and orthodox Christian doctrine, to him also belongs the primacy of "the firstborn over all creation" because "in him all things hold together." In other words, the divine nature manifesting itself in the physical form of Jesus of Nazareth is, in fact, the integrating principle to which all life adheres, the focal point from which all being takes its meaning, the source of all coherence in the universe. He is the reality for which Newton's laws

and Einstein's theory are approximations. He is the fulcrum, the
keystone; in T. S. Eliot's phrase, he is "the still point of the turning world." Around him and him alone all else may be said to
radiate. He is the Cosmic Center.

The apostle Paul's cosmology is curiously ahead of its
time. In 62 A.D., scholars were still under the influence of
Thales of Miletus and Aristotle, though heading toward an explanation that Ptolemy of Alexandria would codify into a system less than a century later. That system would govern astronomy for the next fourteen hundred years. But the Ptolemaic
model was wrong, the Copernican model was wrong, as also
seem to be the modern models proposed or rejected by Einstein,
Lemaitre and Eddington, de Sitter, and Hoyle.

Is it any wonder? Modern theories about the universe
begin by dismissing any thought of a presumed Creator. They
prefer to solve the problem without benefit of any known quantity or quality. Paul's cosmology differs, for he begins from the
known and proceeds on the best possible empirical evidence—
the demonstrable supremacy of Jesus Christ over elements in
both life and death.

His primacy over all created things extends beyond those
creatures and natural objects we behold to include unseen elemental forces of the universe, here called "thrones or powers or
rulers or authorities." As Lord of the universe, nothing is
beyond his control. Again, Teilhard's literal understanding
makes the point explicit. In speaking of "the Universal Christ,"
Teilhard explains,

> By the Universal Christ, I mean Christ the organic
> center of the entire universe, . . . that is to say, the
> center not only of the earth and mankind, but of
> Sirius and Andromeda, of the angels, of all the
> realities on which we are physically dependent.

We don't adequately appreciate the mystery of the Incarnation until we acknowledge the centrality of the Lordship of
Christ. The Word-Made-Flesh is Lord over all those
phenomena of his creation which we identify as gravity or the

twelve-tone scale, which we codify as the laws of thermodynamics or the spectrum of color. Ancient mythologies such as the Greeks' identified and personified forces of nature as, for example, Aeolus, god of the wind, or Poseidon, god of the sea. It's no heresy for us to remember Aeolus and Poseidon, so long as we also remember the One to whom they are subject. For when the wind sweeping down from the Golan Heights had roiled the Sea of Tiberias into a fearful storm, we read in Matthew 8 that the Lord of all creation "rebuked the winds and the waves, and it was completely calm" (Matthew 8:26). He ordered Aeolus, he commanded Poseidon, and they obeyed him. "What kind of man is this?" exclaimed his new disciples. "Even the winds and the waves obey him!" The answer to their question, in Ralph P. Martin's coinage, is that Jesus of Nazareth is "the cosmocratic Christ."

The astonishment of the disciples, like our own reluctance to acknowledge his Lordship, distresses because they had already witnessed the faith of a supposedly pagan Roman officer (Matthew 8:5-13). In humility marked by inspired insight, this Roman soldier, petitioning Jesus for a miracle of healing, discovers truth at its very Center. He recognizes an analogy between his military position and the elemental hierarchies of the universe. He is a man with authority to give orders that must be obeyed; but his authority is limited, for he too is under the authority of higher ranking officers, the provincial governor, the senate in Rome, the emperor Tiberius himself.

By this line of reasoning, the Roman officer has been brought to realize that faith begins with a recognition of the sovereignty of God. He identifies that same sovereignty with the Person of Jesus of Nazareth. To him he ascribes the highest possible authority—even over death itself! He anticipates Jesus' astonishing claim following the Resurrection, "All authority in heaven and on earth has been given to me" (Matthew 28:18). Just as the centurion can issue an order to his subordinates and expect it to be obeyed, so can the Lord Jesus Christ command disease and death and be obeyed. All that's necessary is for him to speak the word.

And he is himself "that Word above all earthly powers," at whose divine summons even the grave must yield. For when the Lord of the universe speaks, what power dares to challenge or to ignore? By his Resurrection, Jesus of Nazareth confirms his rightful claim to Lordship. Yet it's this claim which scandalizes so many. At Christmas, they murmur their adoration for the Baby of Bethlehem, on Good Friday, they weep at the tragic martyrdom of the Teacher. But because they have never recognized that Jesus of Nazareth embodies "the fullness of God," these same sentimentalists become outraged at the preaching of the Resurrection.

It's been a scandal for almost two thousand years, ever since the tiny group of apostles, augmented by a few women, began telling the news, that "the Lord is risen indeed." Thereafter, Paul asserts, the Risen Christ "appeared to more than five hundred of the brothers at the same time, most of whom are still alive, though some have fallen asleep" (1 Corinthians 15:6). These public appearances before eyewitnesses whose testimony could not be invalidated gave incontrovertible proof of the Resurrection. And there was another kind of evidence. So convinced were the few believers in the Resurrection, it turned fearful men into fearless proponents of a new way of living, even at the risk of whipping, imprisonment, and death. Because of their faith, the greatest manhunt in history has gone on for twenty centuries—the search for a man who refuses to stay dead!

Such faith leads to total emancipation from elemental powers, from demonic powers, from bondage to the wheel of fate. Instead, as Henri-Charles Puech puts it, "A straight line traces the course of humanity from initial Fall to final Redemption." The coming of God-in-Flesh gave history a positive meaning, writes D. M. Baillie,

> by producing a real eschatology, a concrete time-scheme, a sacred story, which was firmly connected with history by the conviction that at its central point the Divine had actually come right into history. From that central point faith could look backwards

and forwards, and everything fell into its place in a sacred story whose center was the Christ who had come in the Flesh. Creation, Fall, Promise, Prophecy, the death and resurrection and ascension, the coming of the Holy Spirit, the Church and the spreading of the Gospel, the Second Coming and the final consummation. This is the story that overcame the cyclic view of history, and it all depends on the Christology at the heart of it.

To which we may also add the statement of Paul Tillich:

History and Christology belong to one another as do question and answer. . . . Instead of the beginning and the end of history determining its center, it is its center that determines its beginning and end.

This understanding, that Christ stands at the center of history, delivers the Christian from an otherwise cold, cosmic philosophy, a theology derived from belief in a depersonalized universal magneto. Instead, we worship a God who cares for his cosmos—every distant planet and asteroid, every form of life in whatever galactic shape. We don't know in what form he chooses to reveal himself to distant nebulae; we only know that he isn't aloof, disinterested, or worse, uninterested in the affairs of his creation. Instead, he acts to bring about his divine purposes. Should there be life on any other remote sphere and that life need redemption, the Lord of the universe will act to redeem.

In human experience, the mighty acts of God are manifest by common grace: the phenomena of light by day for work, dark at night for sleep; the cycle of seasons bringing to pass planting, growth, harvest, and recovery; perhaps most important in this sinful realm, restraint of evil keeping back the full measure of human malice and iniquity. God's special grace also reveals his acts on our behalf: the warning of his prophets, witness of his written Word, testimony of his church, and presence of his Spirit.

But the paramount act of God was the Incarnation itself. Through the Person of Jesus, a window was opened so that men could glimpse what God had intended life to be. In seeing Jesus, humanity obtained fulfillment of a prophecy which neither Isaiah nor John the Baptist could have understood, even as they spoke it. But today, in our motorized efficiency, we can! Isaiah's vivid language depicts a topographical problem, leveling the land in order to build a highway:

> A voice of one calling:
> "In the desert prepare
>   the way for the LORD;
> make straight in the wilderness
>   a highway for our God.
> Every valley shall be raised up,
>   every mountain and hill made low;
> the rough ground shall become level,
>   the rugged places a plain.
>
> (Isaiah 40:3-4)

Some eight hundred years later, John the Baptist's challenge to Israel included the prophet's words. They must have seemed strange to pilgrims flocking from Jerusalem to John's desert habitat. Certainly the roads they'd traveled were far from being straight and smooth; no mountain had been leveled, no ravine raised. Their roads were scarcely more than tracks across barren hills and through parched Judean wadis. Even today's tourist on the old road from Jerusalem to Jericho can understand how primitive travel must have been two thousand years ago.

But the prophecy makes sense to us because we know the engineering marvel of modern highway construction. We have the privilege of speeding across the country on a turnpike, an Interstate expressway, and in Britain, a dual carriageway. Isaiah's prophecy foretold a time of direct and ready access to God. Now, John declares, that time has come: "This is the One you've been waiting for!" The appearance of God-in-Flesh overcame every natural obstacle hindering mankind from knowing him. In other words, the Incarnation is God's freeway, and the only toll required is faith.

THE DRAMA OF REDEMPTION

Where does the divine freeway lead? It runs from horizon to horizon, from past to future. Its origins are in alienation from God, but it passes into reconciliation and beckons the traveler onward to ultimate union with God. So Paul declares in the passage following the Incarnation hymn:

> Once you were alienated from God and were enemies in your minds because of your evil behavior. But now he has reconciled you by Christ's physical body through death to present you holy in his sight, without blemish and free from accusation—if you continue in your faith, established and firm, not moved from the hope held out in the gospel. This is the gospel that you heard and that has been proclaimed to every creature under heaven, and of which I, Paul, have become a servant (Colossians 1:21-23).

This passage sums up the cosmic drama of redemption, which in a later paragraph Paul stages like a sanctified *Götterdämmerung*. Except that, in Paul's presentation, a richly ironic reversal occurs: Instead of the Crucifixion meaning a divine demise or "twilight of the gods," it becomes a prelude to ultimate victory. For if the death of Jesus is tragic, his resurrection makes it glorious.

Yet too often the defeat of Satan seems to smack of melodrama—a villain demanding payment of his bond; the helpless victim about to be ravished; the hero achieving a last-minute rescue. If so, it may be because human limitations have never permitted mankind to comprehend the ineffable grandeur of Good or the unspeakable horror of Evil. And so, we've allowed this titanic struggle between Good and Evil to be trivialized into stereotypes of mustachioed villains, fainting victims, and handsome heroes.

There was nothing shallow or cheap about the victory Jesus Christ won through death and resurrection. But there is dramatic irony, and Paul helps us to grasp, if only slightly, the meaning behind the great drama at the Cross.

Following Satan's revolt and defeat in heaven, he waited through aeons for a chance to avenge his loss. At last in Eden, he seized upon an opportunity and by seducing the Woman led humanity into rebellion against God. Again he lost and heard a promise of retribution against himself: The Seed of the Woman would bruise the head of the Serpent, even though the Serpent, in return, would wound her Offspring's heel. Retaliation might have dire consequences for them both, but Satan would prepare to withstand the worst in hopes of winning the best.

At the Incarnation, Satan and his legions laughed that God could have blundered so! For God to reduce himself to weakness and vulnerability in the form of a baby was beyond Satan's comprehension. But he was determined to take full advantage of God's egregious error. Satan wasted no time. The conditions of Jesus' birth exposed him to the dangers of infant mortality; still the Child survived to escape also Herod's maddened slaughter of Bethlehem's innocents, clearly a Satanic stroke. What other perils confronted Jesus in childhood and adolescence, we don't know. But we do know of many incidents during his brief public life whose threat is Satan-inspired.

We also know of instances when Satan's ploy was flattery or the casting of doubt. Most notable among these is the climax of the wilderness temptation. When Jesus refused to submit to any of Satan's blandishments, Luke tells us that "[the devil] left him until an opportune time" (Luke 4:13).

There's something so ominous about that phrase, "until an opportune time," that a balanced mind can scarcely hold it. For Satan, Jesus' refusal to compromise and enter into a pact with him against the Father is the final declaration of war. He retires to await the moment of attack, which, when it comes in condemnation and death, bears all the hallmarks of the Great Deceiver: betrayal by one friend, denial by another, abandonment to the enemy, false accusation resulting in gross injustice, the devaluation of truth to serve the ends of liars. After the collapse of his opposition, Satan's apparent victory must have seemed hollow indeed. Even the Father himself appeared to capitulate and disown the weakling impostor.

But just at the moment of jeering scorn and contempt, when the King of Hell was quivering in anticipation to devour another soul, the Deceiver was himself deceived; at least, that's how Martin Luther expressed it. Satan had failed to recognize, in Jesus of Nazareth, "the fullness of God." He'd made the mistake of allowing the conditional *if* and its concomitant doubts to govern his plan: "*If* you are the Son of God" weakened Satan's respect so that he took his antagonist too lightly. Thus deluded, Satan supposed that Jesus was less than he claimed and therefore assailable. The final cry from the Place of the Skull, "It is finished," was at once Satan's fleeting spasm of ascendancy and the sentence of his eternal doom.

For now Satan would learn the truth and learn it the hard way. Now all fetters of humanness, imposed upon the divine nature of the Incarnate Word, could be shaken off. With them also went the shackles of sin and guilt under the Law borne by mankind since Adam. Paul's electrifying words to the Colossians speak the message:

> For it is in Christ that the complete being of the Godhead dwells embodied, and in him you have been brought to completion. Every power and authority in the universe is subject to him as Head. . . . For he has forgiven us all our sins; he has cancelled the bond which pledged us to the decrees of the law. It stood against us, but he has set it aside, nailing it to the cross. On that cross he discarded the cosmic powers and authorities like a garment; he made public spectacle of them and led them as captives in his triumphal procession (Colossians 2:9-10, 13-15, NEB).

The language here shines with brilliance of metaphors on the grand scale of poetic vision; yet it is language nonetheless to be believed in all its directness and fidelity to the revelation of God in Christ. First, the debtor's bond has been redeemed, paid for by One whose wealth of grace can cancel the debt we owed—a pledge to live under the moral law, an obligation we had neither power nor inclination to keep. Yet Jesus Christ pays that pledge for us, if by faith in him we allow him to do so. Second, the bond itself, the law we couldn't keep, has been crucified. It no longer lives to torment us with our failings. That law is dead so that we—breakers of that law—may live under a new regime of Grace.

The third metaphor shows the Lord of the cosmos asserting his rightful authority over lesser powers to which he had subjected himself in humiliation. Now he rises, as if from a costume in disguise, tosses away with contempt those rags of slavery, and stands forth in all his sovereign splendor. In the final metaphor, Paul uses his readers' knowledge of the Roman conqueror's finest hour, a parade through the streets of Rome to the steps of the Capitol. This march of triumph was granted by the Senate to mark only the most significant military victories. Its rituals were carefully observed. Included in the procession were some of the spoils of victory—treasures, works of art, and prominent prisoners of war, whose execution usually followed the festive event. In making his allusion to a Roman triumph, Paul depicts the conquering Christ, Lord over all Creation, leading his prisoners—those powers that formerly opposed him—in a public display of their submission. He is the invincible Lord.

"The greatest contribution of Christianity," said Nikolai Berdyaev, "consisted in that it liberated man from the power of the baser elemental nature and demons. It did so through the agency of Christ and the mystery of redemption." But how was this liberation achieved? Why was Satan gulled by God's masquerading as a Man? Perhaps the answer is that Satan didn't know everything God knows and wants us to know as well.

THE CENTER INCARNATE

The Christian world-and-life view accepts an assumption—that God sees more than we can because he has the advantage of an all-seeing eye called omniscience. As a corollary, a Christian theory of knowledge must begin by asserting that God knows more than he has ever chosen to share with men. It's one of the privileges of omniscience and infinitude. But, having granted that assumption, Paul tells us that God, remarkably, has disclosed his best secret to men, a secret "hidden for long ages past" (Romans 16:25), ever since by sin Man forfeited the best of his prerogatives as the only creature made in the image of God. That privilege was Man's daily communion with God. But because Man's inordinate pride—his primary sin leading to acts of disobedience—alienated him from God, the human race was punished when God withdrew from men the Word—the single, universal means by which Adam, Cain, Abel, Seth, Enoch, Noah, and his sons had learned to invoke the Lord by name.

From Eden to Babel, human consciousness of God diminished, but after Man's arrogance at Babel, his enmity against God increased. From that moment until the Incarnation, the message of God belonged only to particular men, patriarchs and prophets to whom the Word of the Lord came like purging fire to their unclean mouths. The message from the Lord through the prophets told of a Deliverer promised to Adam's descendants and coming directly from Abraham's line. But this message, as the writer of the Letter to the Hebrews states, had never been given in complete form; rather, it had always been spoken in bits and pieces, as though God had chosen only to offer intimations of his plan to redeem mankind. Then suddenly, at a certain known point in time, the event occurred: God spoke once more, but this time it was the Word himself, the "Son, whom he appointed heir of all things, and through whom he made the universe. The Son is the radiance of God's glory and the exact representation of his being, sustaining all things by his powerful word" (Hebrews 1:2- 3).

It is the great mystery; as C. S. Lewis calls it, "the Grand Miracle." The Incarnation supersedes all we understand about flesh and spirit, illusion and reality. It contradicts the maxim of semantics, that "the *word* is not the *thing*." In this case, the Word is everything! Incarnate as one of us, the Man beyond time yet as one of his time, visible, tangible, glorious in his humanity, gloriously full of the grace and truth that are eternal attributes of God.

The late physicist-philosopher Michael Polanyi spoke of our need to interiorize those things we know, "to pour ourselves into them," because he said, "it is by dwelling in them that we make them mean something on which we focus our attention." If there's to be a simple, straightforward explanation of the Incarnation, this may be it: God became man—the Word became flesh—so that the meaning and value of human existence might be ratified in the experience of God. God chose this means of disclosing himself and then waited and waited, according to his own will and purpose, until the time was ripe. So Paul told his readers at Ephesus,

> And he made known to us the mystery of his will according to his good pleasure, which he purposed in Christ, to be put into effect when the times will have reached their fulfillment—to bring all things in heaven and on earth together under one head, even Christ (Ephesians 1:9-10).

And later, Paul reiterates:

> In reading this, then, you will be able to understand my insight into the mystery of Christ, which was not made known to men in other generations as it has now been revealed by the Spirit to God's holy apostles and prophets. . . . and to make plain to everyone the administration of this mystery, which for ages past was kept hidden in God, who created all things (Ephesians 3:4-5, 9).

As it has now . . . Why now? The question of God's timing has always troubled those who presume to know better. In *Jesus Christ Superstar*, Judas Iscariot asks Jesus,

> Why'd you choose such a backward time and such a
> strange land?
> If you'd come today you would have reached a
> whole nation—
> Israel in 4 B.C. had no mass communication.

But Judas is as wrong in his pop critique as he is wrong in his betrayal. The world of Caesar Augustus was literally spilling over in readiness for some sign, some token of genuine peace that would exceed the *Pax Romana* imposed by military force. It was a world of slavery and oppression, of notorious cruelty and bloodshed.

Ironically, however, the Roman Empire at the birth of Jesus was also brimming over with possibilities for the eventual spreading of his gospel. The Roman eagle had sponsored numerous civilizing advantages under its wingspread. The Mediterranean had largely been freed from piracy; the Roman Empire's remarkable network of highways made itinerant evangelism possible for Paul, Silas, Barnabas, Peter, and others. When they met local opposition, they had the dignity and protection of Rome's system of justice to assist them. Even from their prison cells, these followers of the strange cult known to Romans as "the Name" seem to have been able to rely upon the rights of private correspondence, writings which today comprise the bulk of the New Testament.

In the land of Israel itself, the time was also ripe. Politically, the spirit of the Maccabees continued to incite the guerrilla band called Zealots; at the same time, scholars and ascetics of the Essene sect were promoting the close study of the Scriptures and looking for a literal fulfillment of the old prophecies.

No, Broadway's Judas is wrong. The timing of the Incarnation was no mistake. The whole world was at the ready, in a plethora of expectancy, because, as Paul tells the Galatians, "the time had fully come" (Galatians 4:4). God acted in Jesus Christ at just the right time, choosing to let the human race share his astonishing secret with him.

This secret is Christ himself. As he is Lord of the universe, the Cosmic Center, so he wants to assert his claim over individual men and women—to become Lord of each person and the very Center of each human being. God's secret is his invitation to leave our place, somewhere on the dizzying circumference, to break the centrifugal force driving us away from him, and to find our home at the Center. For there, "in the shelter of the Most High," is the loving protection of the Lord God himself; there too resides freedom from fear, as Psalm 91 promises.

The secret has other surprises. Once we identify Jesus Christ as the Center, says Paul, we discover that "in [him] are hidden all the treasures of wisdom and knowledge" (Colossians 2:3). This is a claim immensely more radical and far-reaching than even the secular assertion of egocentricity. Jesus Christ is the Center; all wisdom and knowledge originate in him; all truth is with him at the Center. But, fused by faith into union with his Lord, a Christian is also at the Center, experiencing what it means to know the meaning of creative and redemptive truth at its core. This Christian claim is all-encompassing, unremitting in its absolutism. It announces, as Calvin Seerveld says, with "scandalous intolerance," that only by confessing that Jesus of Nazareth is also the Incarnate Lord of the universe can we begin to know and understand that universe.

There's no other path to true wisdom, as the Scriptures declare, most imaginatively perhaps in Job 28. There the poet draws his analogy from the act of mining for precious gems:

> Man's hand assaults the flinty rock
>   and lays bare the roots of the mountains.
> He tunnels through the rock;
>   his eyes see all its treasures.
>
> (Job 28:9-10)

But while a man may probe the darkest depths of Earth for gold, silver, and jewels, he can't find the jewel of God's hidden secret, the source of ultimate wisdom; indeed, he has no idea where to look. "We do not obtain the most precious gifts," wrote Simone Weil,

> by going in search of them but by waiting for them. Man cannot discover them by his own powers and if he sets out to seek for them he will find in their place counterfeits of which he will be unable to discern the falsity.

Instead, wisdom must be a gift of God granted through godly fear, an unreserved acknowledgment of the sovereignty of God. This is the beginning of faith which, in turn, is the beginning of wisdom, for

> "The fear of the Lord—that is wisdom,
>   and to shun evil is understanding."
>
> (Job 28:28)

The Christian claim also asserts that when principles of belief in a created cosmos submissive to the Creating Lord are energized, character is altered, behavior is affected, and the sentient spirit of man perceives for the first time a wholeness to replace fragmentation. Integrated with the Center of all truth, one can come to know that, indeed, the whole is greater than the sum of its many parts; that there is meaning to be found, even in the apparent void. In short, when one comes to acknowledge that Jesus is Lord, faith shapes life, and life derives its essence from faith.

These aren't my opinions on the matter. The centrality of the Lordship of Jesus Christ isn't merely one of several options available to the Christian but the categorical imperative derived from the authority of Scripture.

When our older son Don was considering colleges, Lory and I took him on a tour to help him narrow his choices. In Michigan we stood on the campus of a liberal arts college founded in the nineteenth century by one of the strictest Protestant denominations. I asked the college representative about spiritual concerns within the college community and was told that, a few years before, chapel services had been abandoned; shortly after, the office of the chaplain had been abolished, along with courses in religion. Then he must have noted dismay in my face, for he brightened with enthusiasm when he told me, "In place of all that we now offer the Center for Constructive Alternatives."

He had no reply when I asked him, "Alternatives to what?" The only alternative to wisdom is ignorance; the alternative to life is death.

THE MIND OF CHRIST

To live by faith an integrated life, in touch with the very Center of all Being, means that we'll come to know what Paul called "the mind of Christ" (1 Corinthians 2:16). Harry Blamires begins his book, *The Christian Mind*, with an announcement that is all too sadly true: "There is no longer a Christian mind." Certainly, in our secular culture there's no evidence of a Christian mind, a Christian perspective, a Christian criterion. But even within the community of confessing Christians, it's sometimes difficult to discern the presence of a Christian mind— "the mind of Christ."

Surely these ought to be synonymous terms. To speak of the Christian mind ought to evoke in us the mind which was in Christ Jesus, the mind which is the Logos of John 1, the Eternal Wisdom of Proverbs 8. Among many descriptions of the Christian mind, one seems of overriding importance: the mind of Christ as the source of all integrity and wholeness of truth. Because Jesus Christ is truth, the human being of like-mind to Christ stands uniquely within an unbroken web of truth.

This truth shapes the Christian mind, primarily but not exclusively, through study of the written Word. The Christian must be biblically informed; his attitude and actions must take into account what Scripture declares to be mankind's condition before God and God's reconciling grace in Jesus Christ. But the Christian isn't called to be limited to Bible study. An integrated

Christian mind is compelled to study and learn more about human nature and the nature of the universe—to study art, politics, physics, and every other area of human knowledge— because all these belong in the realm where Christ is Lord.

Simone Weil has a striking word on this point. She argues, first, that "prayer consists of attention." But fallible human beings, no matter how devout, lack the discipline of concentration to wait attentively upon God. So the scholar, mystic, and martyr Simone Weil suggests that school exercises—a Latin translation, a geometry problem—be used to train the powers of attention so necessary in prayer. Then she adds this beautiful reflection:

> The solution of a geometry problem does not in itself constitute a precious gift, but the same law applies to it because it is the image of something precious. Being a little fragment of particular truth, it is a pure image of the unique, eternal, and living Truth, the very Truth which once in a human voice declared, "I am the Truth."
>
> Every school exercise, thought of in this way, is like a sacrament.

Here is an example of what Blamires identifies as "thinking Christianly." We might also call it thinking that is *whole* and *wholly* Christian, drawing its critical and discriminating powers from the Lord who is himself the source of all clarity and light. Such thinking must be free from narrow-mindedness, purged of the dross of parochialism or sectarianism, totally open to the truth that sets one free.

Yet both these qualities—an intellect steeped in the Bible and honed to critical keenness—can be ruined if the Christian mind falls prey to pride. The mind of Christ is marked by humility and obedience, qualities particularly important to Christian scholars. The Christian mind cannot admit of arrogance, and the Christian who footnotes himself is at least a questionable scholar. Anyone looking for the capstone to the Christian mind should listen once more to the fifteenth-century monk, Nicholas of Cusa:

> We then, believers in Christ, are led in learned ignor-
> ance to the mountain that is Christ.

To Secular Man, the Christian mind is incomprehensible. He equates humility with Uriah Heep's hypocrisy and misconstrues meekness for weakness. Instead, Secular Man lusts for power. Increasingly, our best-selling books bear titles such as *Go For It!* and *Eat to Win* or *Winning Through Intimidation* and *Power! How to Get It, How to Use It*. These and others like them advocate postures of self-importance and tactics borrowed from jungle warfare. Yet the shallowness and cynicism of the mentality behind these books is well illustrated by a quotation from *Time* magazine's feature story about their authors. Speaking of one of these writers, an acquaintance says, "To know him well is to know he doesn't have much of a center, and so he collects roles." Here, once again, is that appalling inner emptiness so characteristic of Secular Man.

Yet even out of the depths of that spiritual void comes a challenge voiced by Albert Camus:

> What the world expects of Christians is that Chris-
> tians should speak out, loud and clear, . . . in such a
> way that never a doubt, never the slightest doubt,
> could rise in the heart of the simplest man.

Such a challenge, coming as it did from an acknowledged disbeliever, is too compelling to be ignored. It summons every professing Christian to ask himself what he must do to "speak out loud and clear," to answer the deepest questions of the human heart. Of course the Christian knows that he is often victimized by a stammering tongue; he is subject to the limits of language; he can never quite overcome the gulf separating what he is from what he ought to be. Still, the Christian is assured that though he fails, though even heaven and earth should pass away, the Center continues fixed, the Living Word remains. T. S. Eliot wrote in "Ash-Wednesday,"

> And the light shone in darkness and
> Against the Word the unstilled world still whirled
> About the center of the silent Word.

If we believe that the Person of Jesus Christ incarnates the complete being of God, that he is at the Center shaping who we are and what we know, then ought we not by our very bodily presence to be exemplifying—is it too much to say incarnating?— the presence of Jesus Christ?

This is the meaning of the phrase, "the integration of faith and learning." It calls for a correlation between what we believe and how we respond to the world we live in. But integration must never become an evangelical cliche reserved to professional scholars. Instead, there must be an integration of faith with every vocation—the selling of used cars, the making of political decisions. We need an integration of faith and *living*.

Here is the goal that Elton Trueblood calls "the penetration of total life," that Paul calls taking "captive every thought to make it obedient to Christ" (2 Corinthians 10:5). Only when Jesus Christ is given his rightful place at the Center of the universe I inhabit—the universe particular to every individual— can I hope to avoid relapsing into a secular mentality so imperceptible yet so pervasive that it reaches into every corner of my life.

Chapter 5

An Unshackled Universe: The Consummation in Christ

*A*s a teenager in Western Ontario, one of my entertainments was a late Sunday night radio program. It wasn't any of the popular comedians or detective dramas, broadcasts taboo on the Lord's Day. Instead my amusement came from blasphemy. A Detroit station carried the all-night caterwauling from Prophet Jones's Dominion of God, and I was a steady listener.

The Prophet represented himself as an apotheosis, the Messiah (as he often intoned) of the Western hemisphere. His throng of disciples seemed to believe him. One evening, the congregation in his tabernacle must have been so large, a man unable to see the Prophet stood on his chair. Ushers then rushed to seat him, for over the airwaves I heard the voice of Prophet Jones, "Let him be, let him be! They climbed trees to see me when I was here before."

Today's news is full of similarly striking claims. Los Angeles newspapers announce "The 7th Wonder of The Modern World" to be seen at O. L. Jaggers's Universal World Church:

> 7 to 8 P.M. Channel 52. *The person of the Lord Jesus*
> *Christ will appear at the door of the church. The*
> *shekinah glory of God, so thick it obscures the faces*
> *of the great audience, fills the house—never before*
> *televised!*

But before one can recover from that promise, another stunning sideshow pitch:

> *The Mighty Transubstantiation Communion Mir-*
> *acle.* The most beautiful event in the history of man-
> kind! Sunday morning Jan. 18th—10 A.M. More
> than 7000 anointed at the Golden Altar.

> *The Golden Altar of Incense Prayer and the Ark of*
> *the Covenant of Immortality, the splendiferously*
> *beautiful Altar of Prayer with Ezekiel's Wheels upon*
> *it will be unveiled!*

Equally notorious, though less hyperbolic, is the Korean Sun Myung Moon, whose Unification Church has been transplanted here. His sect believes—and Moon's sermons teach—that after mankind's fall into sin, God sent his Son in the Person of Jesus to restore humanity, choosing "the nation of Israel as the landing site for the Messiah." God's preparation also included the Old Testament prophecies and preaching of John the Baptist. But Israel misinterpreted the prophets; John the Baptist bungled his mission: "Jesus seemed to be a loser," says Moon, "and John decided not to side with Jesus. He thought it would be much better to deny everything."

So then, according to Moon, God adopted an emergency program and allowed the crucifixion of Jesus. This revised plan was communicated to Jesus by Moses and Elijah on the Mount of Transfiguration. The result of the Cross is "spiritual salvation only," a ransom paid to Satan by which "God could claim the souls of men, though he could not give redemption of the body."

Only through the Resurrection and Second Coming, Moon declares, may we achieve our physical redemption as well.

America is to be the Messiah's "landing site in the twentieth century." But we must not repeat the error of the Jews two thousand years ago. In their literalism, they misconstrued metaphors predicting the Son of Man's appearance in clouds of heaven. So may we also misinterpret what Moon regards as contradictory imagery and thereby miss the Messiah's return.

In fact, he intimates, most of us have already missed it! For although Moon is too cagey to claim publicly that he is "the Third Adam"—his term for the returning Christ—he allows the gullible to infer, at least, that he is the appointed forerunner, a new John the Baptist. Privately—some of his former converts report—he openly declares himself to be Messiah, his wife is the Bride of Christ; together they are the real parents of all who believe. To insure their eventual share of world domination, Moon's followers must now submit to his iron rule.

Charlatanism, as Jesus told his inquirers, is only one of the signs of the times, "the beginning of birth pains" for the end of the age (Matthew 24:8). Increasing numbers of those claiming to be Christ are a sure indication, according to Scripture, that the end of the age is upon us, the Consummation of the Ages is about to begin. But Jesus also spoke of the disintegration of society as a precursor of the Last Days. Its confirmation in the conditions of modern life lies shattered around us.

To make his point, Jesus gestured toward the great temple, a symbol of solidity and tradition. Then speaking both literally and figuratively, he told his amazed disciples, "Not one stone here will be left on another; every one will be thrown down" (Matthew 24:2). Later, Jesus catalogued the disaster, with civil and international wars, famines and earthquakes—common enough at any period. But their ferocity at the End of Time will lead to widespread personal betrayal until, at last, lawlessness overcomes human compassion and "the love of most will grow cold" (Matthew 24:6-12). Fire and brimstone destroyed Sodom and Gomorrah, it's true; but now at the End, all natural channels of love are to be frozen by selfishness and greed. As if in agreement, Robert Frost writes:

I think I know enough of hate
To say that for destruction ice
Is also great
And would suffice.

According to *The Bulletin of the Atomic Scientists*, September 1984 issue, its Doomsday Clock has once more been moved ahead to read "five minutes before midnight." And in Old Jerusalem, orthodox Muslims have reinforced the walled-up Eastern Gate, fearing Ezekiel's prophecy that God's Messenger, the incarnate glory of the God of Israel, will reenter the Holy City through its Eastern Gate.

To Secular Man, of course, all this talk of Doomsday is so much superstition. Secularism doesn't dispute the fact of our present brokenness, but any explanation for world collapse, any phrase suggesting a terminal point in time by which we must remedy that collapse brings utterances of scorn. Apocalyptic becomes an epithet of derision. The notion of divine intervention into the cosmos is pure science fiction. Instead, secularism looks for other reasons, other remedies.

Everywhere within secular culture today, the cry is the same. Whether one reads radical social reformers or listens to television's pop philosophers, their message is proof enough of the splintering havoc brought by our fascination with power and its lasting imprisonment. Everywhere the call goes up for wholeness—for unbroken relationships between persons; for the sanctity of names rather than identification by number; for a renewal of discourse between human beings instead of communication between computers; for an end to faceless and fragmentary signals that no one knows how to decode.

Prisoners of our secular culture have begun to realize that only if such restoration occurs—an *apokatastasis* to redeem our Humpty-Dumpty existence—can humanity hope to know genuine freedom. As it is, life has been increasingly compartmentalized and departmentalized into pigeonholes and cubicles, little areas of experience cut off from each other, like prison cells of the spirit. In education, for example, specialization in tiny precincts of knowledge all but eliminates exchange except among scholars and leads to a crippling loss of proportion and humility, in view of the larger panoramas of learning.

In his 1940 Phi Beta Kappa address at Yale, Robert Hutchins declared the weakness in education to be the fact that "there is nothing to hold it together." Aldous Huxley once remarked on the deficiencies of modern education and its failure to provide graduates with a necessary sense of wholeness:

> They come out into the world, highly expert in their particular job, but knowing very little about anything else and having no integrating principle in terms of which they can arrange and give significance to such knowledge as they may subsequently acquire.

The same must now be said of secular culture in all its forms. "Nothing to hold it together . . . no integrating principle." Persons without a central stabilizing force in their lives. No core of meaning from which ideas may radiate; hence, no possibility for wholeness because the integrated life is possible only when experience derives from principles, when action finds its roots in faith.

But in its quest for wholeness—for the key piece that will put the jigsaw puzzle together—secularism rejects any suggestion of fixity around known truth. One of the macroculture's neutralizing aims has been to blunt any thrust of philosophical distinctives, to keep all questions of dogma in a state of flux, lest they harden into conviction. Most important, to reshape every critical idea until it conforms to secularism's more comfortable doctrines.

One of these doctrines is that human society, by its own ingenuity and resources, will regain its lost innocence and restore mankind to his primeval state of consciousness. Standing against this myth of cyclic renewal—the chance to start all over again—are Konrad Lorenz and Robert Ardrey, who argue that Homo sapiens has been a murderer from the beginning; to return to humanity's earlier state is to recognize the cave as a slaughterhouse.

Opposing Lorenz and Ardrey are Ashley Montagu, Morton Hunt, and Rene Dubos, who writes,

> Man's propensity for violence is not a radical or a species attribute woven in his genetic fabric. It is culturally conditioned by history and the ways of life.

These observers of human behavior believe passionately in the theory of evolutionary progress, an ever-upward-and-onward estimate of the human condition. Ironically, they seem undeterred by the paradox of trusting fallible men and women to construct infallible social institutions. Again, Dubos:

> We cannot escape from the zoos we have created for ourselves and return to wilderness, but we can improve our societies and make them better suited to our unchangeable biological nature. I do not have much faith in the nineteenth-century version of the perfectibility of man, but I believe deeply in the perfectibility of human institutions.

Nevertheless, Lorenz, Ardrey, Raymond Dart, and others trouble their opponents by reminding them of "innate depravity." When he goes on the attack, in his introduction to *Man and Aggression*, Montagu dismisses the biblical doctrine of sin by a flippant and essentially dishonest use of Scripture. For to demonstrate what he regards as obscurantism, he quotes part, but not all, of Paul's description of the unregenerate man in Romans 7:18-24. But Montagu ends his quotation with the anguished cry, "What a wretched man I am! Who will rescue me from this body of death." He stops short of the apostle's triumphant reply, "Thanks be to God—through Jesus Christ our Lord!" (Romans 7:25).

It makes a cunning rhetorical ploy. But having severed truth from truth, is it any wonder that Montagu should find the Christian statement "so damaging, so pessimistic, so fettering of the human spirit"? How tragic a distortion, when the Christian gospel to man is the message of liberation!

On its own terms, secularism isn't opposed to religion, especially religion diluted of its particular strength, rendered vapid and innocuous. In fact, secularism's co-opting of religion makes possible the apparent anomaly, that the secular world-and-life view should attempt to coexist with things of the spirit. But, of course, this is the era of detente. Secularism can even sponsor a "spiritual summit conference," a religious convocation held in New York City to coincide with the thirtieth anniversary of that most secular of human institutions, the United Nations Organization. The goal of such a meeting—held, curiously enough, in the Cathedral Church of St. John the Divine—was to reaffirm, in the words of anthropologist Margaret Mead, "our common humanity." Quoting Thomas Merton, another speaker called for the recovery of "our original unity." Thus the search for oneness goes on.

But we can't afford to miss the underlying point of secularism's campaign for wholeness and the freedom it brings. To regroup society against further disintegration means carrying us back through transhistorical generations to the Plain of Shinar, there to reenact mankind's egocentric assault against the Idea of the Holy. For it's surely worth remembering that the sin of the men of Shinar wasn't in their industry or imagination in erecting the tower; their sin was the desire to usurp the authority of God, to determine solely their own future without restraint or regard for their position as dependent creatures.

This remains the secular objective today. Again, however, the language of international diplomacy effectively disguises the fact that secular naturalism, with its denial of a personal God incarnate in Jesus of Nazareth, is at war with Christian supernaturalism. There are, of course, modern theologians who have tried to blend secularism with Christianity. Their efforts have been as futile as an alchemist's endeavor to find gold in iron pyrites. Many writers have noted this failure, none more urgently than Robert J. Blaikie in *"Secular Christianity" and God Who Acts*. He puts it this way, bluntly and simply:

> These are the alternatives open today: the secular world-view or the Christian one.

"Secular Christianity," of course, claims to be a bridge between these two: but it is a hollow, false claim. If it is secular, then it is not Christian, for it cannot consistently include even the most fundamental and essential presupposition of all biblical theology—the conviction that God is One who acts with purpose in a personal way in this world.

So Blaikie and others place the burden of proof upon equivocating "secular Christians." They must use what sleight-of-hand they may in convincing a world disordered and strewn in chaos that what is not, is; that what is, is not. To accomplish this, "secular Christians" must also do the service of those whom Macbeth identified as

> these juggling fiends . . .
> That palter with us in a double sense;
> That keep the word of promise to our ear,
> And break it to our hope.

A Conflict of Eschatology

At root, conflict between biblical Christianity and any other teaching is over the old problem of history—its origin and its culmination; in other words, the problem is eschatology: How will Time end and Eternity begin? Christians who accept the authority of Scripture believe that the transcendent God is both Creator and Consummator of history, an active participant in human events. He will bring this drama to its final curtain according to a script known only to himself.

Contrastingly, most other religions appear less concerned with history as a terminating flow of events. Some view history as spatial; others, cyclical. The immanent God they worship may or may not reveal himself in a given epoch. There is no sense of finality to his purposes. He leaves the human race with many clues and hints of his will, with occasional prophets and teachers, avatars or incarnations, from whom we are to discern the right way of living. To believe otherwise, in our sophisticated secular culture, is benighted and anti-intellectual. Susan Sontag expresses the opinion:

> Not surprisingly, contempt for intelligence goes with the contempt of history. And history is, yes, tragic. But I'm not able to support any idea of intelligence which aims at bringing history to an end—substituting for the tragedy that makes civilization at least possible the nightmare or the Good Dream of eternal barbarism.

History, Sontag admits, is tragic, although she seems not to understand why. She ignores the cause-effect relationship of sin and death; she passes by any word of explanation for the fettered condition of mankind in a universe itself subject to bondage. She offers no hope of freedom.

But Christianity, on the other hand, teaches that a definite scenario has been worked out. Jesus delineates the eschatological program, with only the timing left undisclosed. The language is perfectly unambiguous: "And this gospel of the kingdom will be preached in the whole world as a testimony to all nations, and then the end will come" (Matthew 24:14). These are logical processes of order and sequence of events, emanating from a plan—not designed in the futile stupidity of man's intelligence but in Divine Wisdom itself. One step follows another in the historical movement toward redemption and reintegration of a fractured world.

This preaching of the Good News throughout the world must of itself be a sign. Who standing on the side of the Mount of Olives that day could have believed that, within thirty years or so, some of them were to carry the message from Madras to Madrid? What gave them this compelling drive to evangelize the nations? Wasn't it the fact that the gospel was thoroughly grounded in history they themselves had experienced? They were, as Luke calls them, "the original eyewitnesses," possessors of "authentic knowledge" (Luke 1:3-4, NEB). They had come face to face with the single most important question in history, the question from Caesarea Philippi, "Who do you say I am?" (Luke 9:20). The apostles' response remains the historic orthodox answer. "The Christ of God," the Messiah, the Son of the Most High God, the Savior of the world.

But rapid spread of the gospel to all nations has slowed so that today more than two-thirds of the world's population knows nothing about Jesus Christ. At the same time, the church appears to be retreating and retrenching from global missionary concern. Funds dry up, mission stations must be closed, a chauvinistic "know-nothing" attitude claims priority for local programs. What causes this loss of mission? What will be the consequences?

THE PROBLEM OF SYNCRETISM

The early church made apostolic demands upon new converts, requiring them to forsake idolatry with its special feasts and fasts and to turn away from all semblance of devotion to the old forms of religious worship. But as the church dispersed throughout Europe, North Africa, and Asia, some rigidity in these expectations relaxed. In the face of growing barbarian opposition to the gospel, St. Gregory I set forth his "principle of accommodation," in a letter dated 18 July 601. Missionaries were no longer permitted to destroy pagan temples, only the idols in them. "Detach them from the service of the devil," wrote Pope Gregory, "and . . . adapt them for the worship of the true God." He also recommended that Christian festivals be instituted to replace pagan feasts. Precedent could be found some three hundred years earlier, when the church had taken over December 25, Rome's celebration of the winter solstice and the sun's return to strength. The Birth of Christ honored the arrival of the Sun of Righteousness. So too celebration of the Resurrection in early spring, which in Britain replaced a feast in homage to Eostre, the Anglo-Saxon goddess, from whose name we derive Easter.

This principle of accommodation had also already been in force in Byzantine Christendom since at least 426 A.D. When

Emperor Theodosius II closed pagan temples, he excepted the Parthenon in Athens, leaving it renamed as "the church of Holy Wisdom"—an accommodation to the principal attribute of the city's patron goddess. But a hundred years later, Emperor Justinian I began construction of a great new cathedral for Constantinople, the Hagia Sophia or "Holy Wisdom." Jealous for the name of his new basilica, Justinian changed the Parthenon's Christian name. This time it became "the church of St. Mary the Virgin," a reminder of Athena's reputation as the virgin goddess. So a pagan temple retained its influence over the church that had supplanted it.

During the age of exploration, accommodation sometimes became indistinguishable from compromise. The conquistador allowed the Cross to accompany him, but his primary objective was to find the Land of El Dorado. The French voyageur sought the Northwest Passage; he tolerated the presence of the black-robed fathers. In this hostile climate, intensified by the ravaging opportunism of their countrymen, European missionaries labored hard to "Christianize" native tribes; but they often found it prudent not to compel every indigenous practice to be abolished. Today travelers throughout Latin America, for example, may visit Roman Catholic churches, where after mass has been said, priests retire and ancient shaman rites begin.

But at least the representatives of Christ retire. In other parts of the world, pagan rites blend with Christian at the same altar until doctrine becomes a melange of the gospel overlaid by animism, ancestor worship, idolatry, and tradition whose origins no one can recall. Throughout South India, for instance, are shrines which to the passerby are neither distinctively Christian nor Hindu. "This is the glory of our Indian faith," an Indian Jesuit tells me. "The face of Christ is the face of a Hindu saint."

The Jesuit refers to his *syncretism*, a distortion of the principle of accommodation. Syncretism isn't a new phenomenon. It has robbed Jesus Christ of his rightful Lordship almost from the beginning of the church. Paul addresses the problem in several of his letters, notably Colossians, where he tells new believers that their old pagan practices are to be discarded now as "a shadow of the things that were to come" (Colossians 2:17).

Clearly, their pagan rituals, insofar as they foreshadow the redemptive work of Jesus Christ, had been of some value. These rites kept reminding the Colossians of their need for a Redeemer. But, says Paul, what use is there now for shadows, for images? The substance of truth itself has been revealed; in Paul's terms, "the reality, however, is found in Christ" (Colossians 2:17). This reality, delineated in the Person of Jesus of Nazareth, can only become blurred and confused if blended with lesser philosophies. Moreover, once Jesus Christ is known and his claims acknowledged, any conscious attempt at syncretism is tantamount to blasphemy because it deliberately withholds from Jesus Christ his rightful supremacy.

Nor is syncretism excusable as the means to a worthy end. Whatever may have been its failures—and there are also successes to be mentioned later—the principle of accommodation has always had higher motives than syncretism. Paul explains to his readers at Corinth,

> To those not having the law I became like one not having the law (though I am not free from God's law but am under Christ's law), so as to win those not having the law. To the weak I became weak, to win the weak. I have become all things to all men so that by all possible means I might save some (1 Corinthians 9:21-22).

Accommodation adapts to new circumstances, new morals, without changing the dynamic character of its message. The package—even the shape of the package—may change, but its contents remain constant. Accommodation is method, but syncretism sucks the marrow from the message. Through syncretism's adulteration, the *kerygma* or proclamation of the gospel loses its power.

Syncretism's starting point is its denial of God's exclusively infallible revelation in Jesus Christ and in the written Word. Whenever a lower view of Jesus Christ and of Scripture creeps into the church, shared revelation with any teaching purporting to be true becomes possible. Since the 1928 World Missionary Conference in Jerusalem, syncretism has been an accepted goal for liberal Christian mission. The final report of that conference declared,

> The task of the missionary today . . . is to see the best in other religions, to help the adherents of those religions to discover, or to rediscover, all that is best in their own traditions, to cooperate with the most active and vigorous elements in the other traditions in social reform and in the purification of religious expression. The aim should not be conversion.

And what do we find a half-century later? Among "secular Christians" in the West and nominal Christians from non-Western nations looking for an ethnic theology, another shift is occurring in the status accorded to Jesus of Nazareth. In one sense, he participates as God's Messenger; he may even be known as Lord. But he loses the uniqueness of his position and becomes instead a cultural symbol, a local deity, a demigod limited in time and place to the Roman provinces at the beginning of the Common Era. The searing words of this Judean radical are memorable; but he transcends time and place only by his lasting influence upon the lives of those who follow his teaching. He becomes merely one of many manifestations of "the Christ-event," one of numerous avatars of "the Cosmic Christ," seen at various times in various forms all over the globe—now Vishnu, now Buddha, now Jesus, now Muhammad, now Sri Ramakrishna, Mahatma Gandhi, Albert Schweitzer, Mother Teresa, and on and on. He is hailed, in Father Raimundo Pannikar's words, as "the Unknown Christ of Hinduism," whom Hindus may worship along with their 330 million other gods.

In nations newly delivered from imperialism and looking for ethnic identity, it's not unusual to find elements of paganism being introduced as evidence of patriotism. Frightened at appearing to be a supporter of a religion yoked with past political oppression, a Western missionary allows the Person of Jesus Christ to be stripped of authority, the gospel to become an empty shell. The result is a potpourri of jingoism and heathen ritual corrupting whatever Christianity is left.

The next logical step from compromise and syncretism gives the broadest possible latitude to any expression of belief. Because all truth is God-given, any semblance of truth testifies of God's presence. "I saw my risen Lord," wrote E. Stanley Jones in *The Christ of the Indian Road*, "entering behind closed doors once again and showing his hands and his side and speaking peace to disciples I had not known." Dr. Jones refers to devout Hindus whose compassion made them appear Christ-like. Another supporter of this opinion, Geoffrey Parrinder, writes,

> If all things subsist in Christ, as the apostle says, then it is Christ and no other who leads men everywhere to salvation. This is the truth that the Gita had adumbrated. Whatever truths there are in Hinduism come from Christ, and any devout prayer and worship are his.

Parrinder goes on to cite Augustine as favoring the view that devout pagans before the Incarnation shared "the reality which we now call the Christian religion." By extrapolation, Parrinder is able to reason that devotion is similarly efficacious today.

This heterodoxy stands opposed to historic declarations of the church, both in Scripture and in documents such as the Thirty-Nine Articles of 1576 or the Westminster Confession of 1646. The Confession reads,

> Much less can men, not professing the Christian religion, be saved in any other way whatsoever, be they ever so diligent to frame their lives according to the light of nature, and the law of that religion they do profess. And to assert and maintain that they may, is very pernicious, and to be detested. (Chapter X, iv)

And Article XVIII states,

> They also are to be had accursed that presume to say,
> that every man shall be saved by the law or sect
> which he professeth, so that he be diligent to frame
> his life according to that law, and the light of nature.
> For Holy Scripture doth set out unto us only the name
> of Jesus Christ, whereby men must be saved.

Edward H Browne, in his *Exposition of the Thirty-Nine Articles*, points out that Article XVIII is addressed not to devout pagans but to complacent believers whose "cold indifference to faith and truth . . . would rest satisfied and leave them in their errors, instead of striving to bring them to faith in Christ." Browne turns the charge of latitudinarianism into an accusation of laziness. It's simply easier to allow men to believe whatever they will than to evangelize them.

But the ultimate controversy concerns universalism, an opinion held by those like John A. T. Robinson, who claims that God is too loving to condemn anyone to eternal separation from himself; or Nels Ferre, for whom God is too powerful to be opposed forever by those who at present reject him. Robinson argues in a famous debate with Thomas Torrance,

> In a universe of love there can be no heaven which
> tolerates a chamber of horrors, no hell for any which
> does not at the same time make it a hell for God. He
> cannot endure that— for that would be the final
> mockery of His nature—and He will not.

And with his characteristic heightened language, Ferre says, "God will put the screws on hard enough to make men want to change their ways, precisely because He loves them enough to do so."

The question of universalism is a serious matter for later discussion. But just at the moment I want to return to an earlier point.

ACCOMMODATION WITHOUT COMPROMISE

There is no absolute connection between the principle of accommodation and heresy. In his *History of Christian Missions*, Bishop Stephen Neill recounts a narrative of great courage and commitment based upon an accommodation to human sacrifice. In the year 1004, heathen priests in Iceland determined to offer two men from each quarter to appease their gods, angered at the spread of Christianity in their land. Upon hearing this, two Christians named Hialte and Gizor called others together and vowed to offer as many men as the pagans. "The heathen sacrifice the worst men," said Hialte, "and cast them over the rocks or cliffs, but we will choose the best men and call it a gift of victory to our Lord Jesus Christ." Hialte and Gizor were themselves the first volunteers.

In Japan, the history of Christian missions dramatically illustrates the principle in a positive light. At the same time that Spanish and French missionaries were encountering the peoples of the New World, a band from the newly founded Society of Jesus arrived on the other side of the globe. These were Francis Xavier and his colleagues, Cosme de Torres and Juan Fernandez. As missionaries in Goa, Portugal's colony on the west coast of India, they had met a Japanese fugitive and converted him. He assured the Jesuits that Japan was a ready harvest for the "Kirishitan" gospel. On 15 August 1549, Francis Xavier and his coworkers arrived on Kyushu, Japan's southernmost island.

Japan's soil proved fruitful indeed for evangelism, and in just twenty-five years, some 100,000 converts had been won. Christian schools and seminaries had been opened under the protection of a ruler named Oda Nobunaga, and in the sacred city of Kyoto a church had been built. By the end of the sixteenth century—in just fifty years time—scholars estimate that Christians may have numbered more than a quarter-million.

Why was St. Francis so successful in his mission? Stephen Neill suggests that the Jesuit, who had previously worked both in Goa and in Macao, recognized in Japan a different culture, a different ground upon which to lay the foundations of faith.

Now that he was confronted by a civilization with so many elements of nobility in it, he saw that, while the Gospel must transform and refine and recreate, it need not necessarily reject as worthless everything that has come before.

These very qualities of nobility, perseverance, and fidelity which characterized Japanese culture were soon to be consecrated in martyrdom for the sake of Jesus Christ. For in 1587, Japan's most powerful ruler, frightened by the Christians' growing influence, expelled the missionaries. None of the seventy or so Europeans left; instead, they went underground and maintained a crypto-Christian church with such intrigues as pretending to conduct Buddhist rites. The price for being discovered was high: In 1597, nine priests and seventeen Japanese were crucified at Nagasaki. Over the next 250 years, Christians endured unspeakable torture until, in 1865, Japan was once again opened to the West, and her Christians came out of hiding.

Their story during those centuries of stifled faith has best been described by Michael Cooper, S. J., and William Johnston, S. J., both of Sophia University, Tokyo, and by the remarkable Japanese novelist, Shusaku Endo. His novel *Silence* is a complex psychological study of trust in the midst of perfidy, of misplaced pity that robs heroic believers of their martyrdom. It's also a compelling statement of the inherent problem in cross-cultural evangelism—the problem of relationships between culture and the Lord Jesus Christ. For Japan is a nation where no dishonoring act can ever be justified, no matter how one rationalizes by the standards of situation ethics. When in the novel a missionary chooses to spit and trample upon a copper medallion bearing the face of Christ, he does so for the most moral reasons—so that his Christian brothers and sisters, his Japanese converts, might be released from hideous torture. But

as the missionary recants, Shusaku Endo calls him to account
with these words: "Dawn broke. And far in the distance the cock
crew."

Still, the faith of those who suffered in Japan was like the
mustard seed or the yeast in Jesus' parables of the Kingdom.
Hidden for two-and-a-half centuries, this faith would not die.
When Japan reentered the community of nations, a few priests
were allowed to minister to diplomats and businessmen. One of
these, Father Bernard Petitjean, reopened the church in
Nagasaki, where one day in 1865, a group of women sought him
out and told him their story. Father Cooper, writing in *The
Japan Times*, brings his account to its climax:

> And so the amazing story of the secret Christians,
> who had tenaciously clung to their religion for more
> than two centuries, gradually came to light. On
> further investigation, small clusters of such Chris-
> tians were discovered in the mountainous districts of
> Kyushu and on the small neighboring islands. The
> Christian message had been carefully handed down
> from father to son through eight or nine generations.
> A special village official was appointed to administer
> baptism, another was in charge of the church calen-
> dar and announced the different feast days. Prayer
> meetings were held at night behind locked doors,
> statues and rosaries were hidden away under the
> floor. Statues of the Buddhist deity Kannon were
> used to represent Our Lady.
>
> Inevitably, in the course of two centuries cut off
> from the outside world, the Christian beliefs of these
> uneducated farmers and fishermen had absorbed
> Shinto and Buddhist elements, but in most cases the
> essentials of Christian teaching still remained. Once
> they had the opportunity and freedom of worship
> was guaranteed by the government, about half of the
> so-called Old Christians established contact with the

returned missionaries and rejoined the visible Church.

This saga continues into our own times, for during its years of conquest, Imperial Japan once again forbade the propagation of the gospel and punished confessing Christians. Then came the atomic bomb and surrender, followed by General Douglas MacArthur's challenge to the church to evangelize Japan. When missionaries arrived in 1946, some of their first apparent converts may have been merely polite Japanese showing obeisance to their conquerors' gods. But once again, from out of hiding, came those genuine believers who had preserved the integrity of the gospel in spite of necessary accommodation to criminal conditions.

In other parts of the world, preaching the gospel presumably for the first time has stirred up ashes of faith and found a spark in memory. The readiness with which some tribes receive the Good News assures an evangelist that the soil has been prepared at some time long past. This *preparatio evangelica* is demonstrated over and over again. In the hill tracts of Bangladesh, an Indo-Burmese tribe known as the Murungs have been responding to the Word of God because, for many generations, they have been looking for just such a Holy Book. According to their traditions, they once possessed a message from God written on banana leaves. But a cow ate it, robbing them ever since of its revelation, until messengers of Jesus arrived. Who is to say this primitive story may not somehow be true?

The idea of a *preparatio evangelica* weaves through the whole history of the church. In the Old Testament, we read of men and women who had never before heard the name of Jehovah nor celebrated the Passover; their faith, however, in One Supreme God was nonetheless confirmed when, like Rahab in Jericho, they met representatives of Jehovah. Judaism itself is preparation for belief in the Messiah, the Lamb of God. Likewise, in the New Testament, we read about Cornelius, Lydia, and the man of Ethiopia, each of whom had been prepared in advance of hearing the gospel.

Simone Weil accounts for the Ethiopian's immediate responsiveness by reminding us that Ethiopia is known to readers of the *Iliad* as "the chosen land of the Gods, the country where, according to Herodotus, adoration was offered to Zeus and Dionysus alone," rather than to the whole pantheon of paganism. From the mythic religion of his own people, the royal steward had already turned to the prophets of Israel and the worship of Jehovah at Jerusalem. All that the evangelist Philip needed, then, was to show how Jesus of Nazareth fulfilled the prophecy of Isaiah. In the Ethiopian's own mind he could make connections between Philip's preaching about Jesus and the mythic foreshadowing of Dionysus's sacrifice. The result was instant faith and obedience.

Such preparation for the seed is the work of the Holy Spirit, the Divine Light "that gives light to every man" (John 1:9). To whatever degree a human being is aware of spiritual reality and thereafter drawn towards the Idea of the Holy, the Spirit of God is responsible. The church has acknowledged this as truth down through the ages since the apostles and fathers, such as Justin Martyr in the second century, expressed it. We have the testimony of believers today who recognize out of their past experience strivings after God. Yet the impetus came not from within themselves; rather, they had been drawn, as if by a giant lodestone, to seek and then to find.

Bishop Lesslie Newbigin, writing out of his many years of observation in South India, refers to new converts' "strong conviction afterwards that it was the living and true God who was dealing with them in the days of their pre-Christian wrestling." And Jacques Maritain has said, "Under many names, names which are not that of God, in ways only known to God, the interior act of a soul's thought can be directed towards a reality which in fact truly may be God."

Perhaps the most striking example from Scripture of ground prepared for evangelism appears in Acts 17. Midway between the main entrance to the acropolis and the agora or marketplace of Athens rises a rocky outcropping known to the world as the Areopagus—the Hill of Ares or, to the Romans, Mars' Hill. Here, tradition tells us, the Greek god of war was tried by his peers, the gods of Olympus, for slaying Poseidon's son. From earliest recorded times, the Hill of Ares served as a meeting place for the council of Athens. Fittingly, in the myth of Orestes, murderer of his faithless mother Clytemnestra, the son appeals to the Areopagites to deliver him from a curse that permits the Furies to pursue him. Solon sat in judgment on the Areopagus; the noble Pericles reconstituted its authority as a homicide court. So it remained throughout the rule of Rome.

But the Areopagus is best known today because to its court a Greek-speaking Jewish lawyer with Roman citizenship argued the case against secularism and idolatry. His brief was eloquent, and we'll come to it presently, but it would have been far less effective had it not been for the *preparatio evangelica* which the apostle found and to which he accommodated his preaching.

The author of the Book of the Acts describes Paul as "greatly distressed" by the multiplicity of idols throughout the city of Athens. His indignation first takes expression in his typical manner of debate with Jews and proselytes in the Athenian synagogue. From there, it spills over into the market square, involving not only casual passersby but also students and teachers from various schools of philosophy located thereabouts— Epicureans and Stoics, for example. Paul's argument, as always, centers on the Resurrection. To some of his listeners, his message is simply ludicrous, for while certain modes of Greek thought included immortality of the soul, none allowed for a bodily resurrection. Yet these intellectuals are at least interested enough to arrange for a public lecture. Perhaps some of them supposed that they were setting themselves up for further amusement; possibly others were sincere about wishing to hear any new thought.

At any rate, Paul accepts their invitation to address the citizens of Athens from the platform of the city's highest court. But by the time he begins his remarks, his approach to the Athenians has changed. He no longer shows outrage at their idolatry; instead, he commends their religious concern as evidence that they are "uncommonly scrupulous" (NEB). The altar inscribed "To an Unknown God" is proof. This is the soil in which to plant the seed: "Now what you worship as something unknown I am going to proclaim to you" (Acts 17:23).

Paul's argument is on behalf of God the Creator, who transcends "temples built by hands," who needs nothing from men. This God calls us to know him personally, says Paul; then quoting the poet Epimenides, a name familiar to Athenians, he suggests an integral relationship of offspring to parent. But though such a Deity has the right to command his creatures to pay him homage, Paul reasons that any gross representation in idols diminishes his glory. Worship of the Creator must be appropriate.

But even at the point of exposing their failure, Paul doesn't condemn the Athenians. His tone now is wholly different from his argumentative exchanges in the agora. He conciliates his audience by informing them that God has chosen to disregard their past practices as done in ignorance. "But now he commands all people everywhere to repent" (Acts 17:30). Repentance in this case specifically means rejecting the worship of idols—the thousands of statues in Athens, particularly the gigantic statue of Athena, carved by Pheidias and overlaid with the golden robe weighing forty talents, which stood in the Parthenon.

Then Paul strikes with the audacity of General Doolittle's raid on Tokyo. He attacks directly the sophistry and cynicism, the egocentricity and secularity within his audience by announcing that God the Creator is also God the Magistrate: "For he has set a day when he will judge the world," says Paul (Acts 17:31). This judgment is to be just; the judge has been divinely appointed; and "he has given proof of this to all men by raising him from the dead."

What a rhetorician! He has brought to the very seat of learning and oratory a model of its highest form. He has chosen the rostrum of Athens's highest court from which to speak concerning matters of ultimate judgment. He has accommodated his presentation perfectly to the emotional and physical circumstances of his audience, building from their experience to his own a bridge which they can readily cross. And then, without compromise, Paul of Tarsus charges them with truth.

The results are what every evangelist must learn to expect. Some scoffed, some evaded the issue by putting it off until another time; but some also believed, including a member of the Court of Areopagus named Dionysius. To this day a church in his name stands at the base of Mars' Hill.

THE MYSTERY OF REDEMPTION

A few years ago, my family and I accompanied my sister Jean and her missionary colleague Lynn Silvernale on a trek into the hill tracts of Bangladesh, beyond Chittagong. By Land Rover, by foot, by poling for hours up the Matumahari River, and then again by foot, we reached the most isolated place I may ever see. It's an indigenous community of Indo-Burmese tribespeople. Their manner of life is as primitive as the Bronze Age. Few of them had ever seen more than a score of strangers; few of them had been beyond the nearest market village called Lama. Almost none of them had seen a motor vehicle—although Chinese jets on reconnaissance flights are becoming less frightening to them.

Among the cluster of huts built from woven matting, my wife and daughter met an old Tipperah woman, who asked thirteen-year-old Ellyn where her husband was. Ellyn smiled but could make no reply because she hadn't understood the question spoken in a foreign tongue. The old woman repeated her question at higher volume, and when the young girl remained silent, the old woman shouted at her, supposing her to be deaf. Then my sister, speaking to the Tipperah woman in a dialect they could both understand, tried to explain. The old woman—like the slave Jim arguing with Huckleberry Finn over a Frenchman's humanity—wasn't convinced.

Along the way to her tribal village, we'd passed through many remote settlements where our very presence was cause for wonderment. A human telegraph system sped before us to alert each household to the spectacle coming down the path—a party of *forengees*. We'd seen malnourished children and lethargic adults, most of them in the perpetual squatting position of the Indian subcontinent, waiting for something to happen. Perhaps we were that something! Hour by hour, I'd felt a growing constriction about my heart, a choking lump in my throat. The extent of human need was obvious all around me, and I was so helpless.

But what of the greater spiritual need? The old tribal woman's ignorance tore into my soul. If she couldn't understand differences in speech—not to mention any difference in marriage customs—how could she possibly be held accountable for understanding that her animism is hateful to God? How could she be condemned for never having trusted in One whose name she may have never heard?

At that moment, questions of universalism, which had never before presented themselves to me in flesh-and-blood, began to trouble me. What if Philip had never met the Ethiopian and told him about Jesus? What if Paul had never introduced the Athenians to their Unknown God? Wouldn't the fullness of God's mercy apply to any honest seekers such as these? Doesn't the promise of a restored universe—an *apokatastasis* such as Peter foretells in Acts 3:21—imply a cosmic redemption? Or can it be possible that acts of human will can eternally resist God's grace?

I freely admit that I have no reasoning power capable of answering these questions. To me, the problem is almost as great a mystery as the Incarnation itself. Yet I'm equally troubled by those Christians who speak so glibly, so unhesitatingly, either for or against some form of universal salvation, as though no mystery exists.

But it does exist, complicated in part, of course, through a confusion of terms. Universalism is not the same as universal salvation, which describes the power inherent in divine atonement to save the entire universe from its lost condition. As such, universal salvation is a teaching well grounded in Scripture, and the sole common ground for any discussion of universalism must also be the authority of Scripture.

The second-century church father Irenaeus declared, "Scripture has given us all the knowledge that is necessary for salvation, and any questions that are not fully answered by Scriptures must be left severely alone." Yet most arguments concerning universalism result in stalemate precisely because one citation from Scripture seems to counter another in the great game of prooftexting. Without wishing to repeat that error, therefore, let's ask what seem to be the essential teachings and their points of differing interpretation.

Scripture teaches that man is alienated from God by sin and must be reconciled to him. Reconciliation has been made possible through faith in the Incarnation and Jesus Christ's atoning death; then confirmed through his Resurrection and Ascension. This reconciliation has been offered to all mankind because the atoning death of Jesus Christ is efficacious throughout the whole creation. Reconciliation exists now for those who believe and thereby come to know the experience called "peace with God through our Lord Jesus Christ" (Romans 5:1). A broader reconciliation that includes liberating the whole cosmos awaits the Second Coming of Christ. On these matters most Christians with a high view of Scripture will agree.

But they disagree vehemently as to how inclusive, how complete, must be the mercy and grace of God in granting salvation. For universalism means to leave no one outside the final forgiveness of God. In effect, universalism says that God will allow no one to be eternally lost from his presence.

Accordingly, almost any discussion of universalism brings accusations of heresy from both sides. "Universalism . . . cannot be supported from Scripture and is a heresy," wrote Harold J. Lindsell in his study paper for the 1974 International Congress on World Evangelization at Lausanne. Of such certainty John Baillie has said that if there were any whom Jesus seemed to exclude utterly from a place among the righteous, "it was those who were so sure that others were excluded."

Dispute over universalism begins with the Greek word *apokatastasis* implying a universal restoration to health or return to a previous state of favor. The *Oxford Dictionary of the*

Christian Church defines *apokatastasis* as "the doctrine that ultimately all free moral creatures will share in the grace of salvation." Perhaps this definition provides a basis for argument. If mankind has been created with free moral agency, including the power of contrary choice, then isn't man free to reject God's offer of reconciliation? Yes, says Lindsell. Universalism violates the choice of those who would prefer separation from God; it turns God into "a capricious being and man a virtual automaton," writes Lindsell.

But others disagree. "I cannot believe," said F. D. Maurice, "that He will fail with any at last; if the work was in other hands it might be wasted; but His will must surely be done, however long it may be resisted." Wrong, says Thomas Torrance. Judas didn't find Jesus' love irresistible—although no one, including Professor Torrance, can rightly claim to know what thoughts beyond remorse Judas may have experienced, even while in the act of suicide. Torrance appears to oppose universalism, however, on larger grounds than quibbles over Judas's possible repentance. He sees universalism as depending on the strength of human reason. It's unreasonable, says the universalist, to assume that God will allow any of his creatures to be separated from him; it's unreasonable to limit God by manifestations of human stubbornness. All this, Torrance would contend, misses the point.

> Universalism is the doctrine that rationalizes sin, that refuses to admit in its dark fathomless mystery a limit to reason. Universalism means that the contradiction can be bridged by reason after all, and constitutes therefore the denial of atonement and the anguished action of Calvary.

G. C. Berkouwer recognizes a somewhat different slant to universalism. He admits that "universalism does not wish to deny the guilt of sin or weaken the wrath of God. But it sees sin and wrath as temporary." Berkouwer also cuts away the ground from those who argue that God's justice demands vindication. Against what he calls "an unbiblical concept of God,"

Berkouwer shows that "God's justice is revealed on the cross," where Jesus Christ bears all the suffering for sin. So, Berkouwer warns,

> in criticizing universal reconciliation, one must be careful not to mount an attack that assails reconciliation itself and eclipses the view of the totally surprising, unexpected aspect of the divine reaction to guilt, rebellion, estrangement, lawlessness, and fall.

The element of surprise! Isn't this, perhaps, the note to strike? The possibility of a gesture by God so astonishing, it knocks all our theories into discard! For doesn't John Newton remind us that there will be three wonders in Heaven: people there we didn't expect to see; people not there we had expected to see; "and wonder of wonders," wrote the one-time slaveship captain, "I shall be there!"

So far, our glimpse at the conflict between particular salvation and universalism has considered only those who have been told "that God was reconciling the world to himself in Christ." Of them, the argument may be simply stated: One side says they are lost because they wish it so; the other agrees with John Baillie, that even those who "deny God with the top of their minds" must believe "from the bottom of their hearts," and so be reconciled eventually by his irresistible grace. We find this paradox in the thinking of Augustine, who opposed universalism yet couldn't get away from believing that God's grace "unfailingly attains its object." And so the conundrum remains.

But what of those who have never heard the gospel, to whom the name of Jesus of Nazareth is even less familiar than that of John Lennon? Are these ignorant, benighted human beings also lost, like those who willfully reject Christ? Or are they to be included among those who will be reconciled when cosmic redemption is at last achieved?

Contrary to some evangelical critics, this doctrine of cosmic redemption isn't an invention of the World Council of Churches. It bears the same warrants from Scripture we claim for personal redemption. The same God who promises the

Woman that from her seed will come forth an Offspring to strike at the Serpent also declares him to be the Incarnate Lord of the cosmos. Through him mankind receives both personal reconciliation with God and a restored universe—a peaceable kingdom where beasts and children play together, where nature is at rest, where storms and earthquakes are forever pacified, where death is known no more, where culture and civilization are integrated in the City of God.

In his essay, "Cosmic Christ and Cosmic Redemption," James P. Martin says,

> Salvation must speak about this fundamental, inescapable fact of the universal destiny of the cosmos. If therefore Jesus Christ is the cosmic redeemer, the scandal of the once-for-allness of his life, death, and resurrection breaks out in new power. The folly of Christ crucified is a cosmic, not a provincial, folly. It is therefore the wisdom of God for his cosmos.

Martin has made an essential point. Cosmic redemption appears to be limited by history to a specific instant in time. It happened, as the Creed declares, "under Pontius Pilate"—never before, never since. The atoning death and glorious resurrection are events in time, and as such may speak continuously to those of us able to look back at them.

But what of those aeons of time preceding the historical event? In strictly human terms, the Cross and Resurrection are *a posteriori* to Julius Caesar, Alexander the Great, Themistocles, Ozymandias, or Sargon. Jesus of Nazareth lived and died more than two thousand years after the pharaohs of Egypt's eleventh dynasty. Yet the gospel teaches that the redemptive work of Christ applies to every member of the human race. A mighty act of God was needed—an act so cloaked in mystery we hear few sermons about it. Yet both Paul and Peter speak of it; the Apostles' Creed says, "He descended into Hell"; the church through the Middle Ages knew it as "the harrowing of Hell."

Admittedly, biblical teaching on this profound topic is incomplete, leaving many questions unanswered. What we know comes from three principal passages: the prophetic Psalm 68, with its references to epic combat between God and his enemies, followed by pictures of triumphant procession; Paul's quotation of this psalm in Ephesians 4:7-10; and the startling words in 1 Peter 3:19-22 and 4:6.

Some theologians have argued that the descent into Hell is a metaphor to depict the anguish of the Cross. We hear a similar hyperbole today: "I went through Hell to get my tax return done on time." Others ascribe symbolic value to the teaching, saying either that Christ bore the sins of humanity to Hell or that in Hell Christ literally fulfilled the prophecies of Genesis 3:15 and Psalm 68:21-23 by crushing the head of the Serpent, the Dragon. Still others see the mystical event as the deliverance from eternal death of God-fearing men and women, those who had lived by faith before the Incarnation.

All these interpretations have value, but a fourth must not be disallowed. For those "spirits in prison" to whom, Peter tells us, Jesus "went and preached" included not only men and women of faith, not only virtuous pagans, but also sinners! Peter does not shy away from direct reference to those whose rebellion against God had scorned the safety of Noah's ark. To them as well the Crucified Redeemer discloses himself. "Why was the Gospel preached to those who are dead?" Peter asks, then answers his own question: "In order that, although in the body they received the sentence common to men, they might in the spirit be alive with the life of God" (1 Peter 4:6, NEB). Can it be that these rebels in life received the mercy of God through Jesus Christ in death? Could the Italian government today pass a decree absolving Brutus and Cassius of their treason in 44 B.C.?

The mystery is too confounding. It is "God's secret wisdom, a wisdom that has been hidden," as Paul writes in 1 Corinthians 2:7. All mankind, it appears, has been provided for in the single, inimitable act of the Incarnation. God cannot be limited

to the ages known as Time; he works his will from Eternity to
Eternity, redeeming, reconstituting, restoring what has been his
from the beginning.

But does this also mean that all mankind shall be saved?
Before we leap to that assumption, Allan D. Galloway offers
this caution. Speaking in *The Cosmic Christ* of those who cannot yet be numbered among believers in Jesus Christ, Galloway
says, "There is no point in going on to discuss the doctrine of
cosmic redemption until they know something of the living experience of personal redemption." One doctrine doesn't super-
sede another; they are, instead, complementary mandates from
God. We aren't empowered to alter Scripture so that the primacy of one teaching is established over another, not even for
the best of human reasons—that is, to make the gospel appealing and acceptable to as many people as possible. The gospel
must remain foolish to those who find it so.

But we still haven't addressed the principal question: Are
the heathen lost?

In the dining commons at Lausanne's Congress, I introduced myself to a village pastor from Papua New Guinea,
seated across from me. As we ate, he told me that he had been
one of the first converts in his tribe. His father had been a
headhunter.

"Did your father ever come to believe in Jesus?" I asked.

"The missionaries had not come yet," he replied.

"May I ask," I inquired as gently as I knew how, "the state
of your father's soul?"

The pastor lifted his head—his face bearing scars of tribal
markings—and addressing me in full voice said, "He is damned
in Hell."

His certitude chilled me. For my part, I couldn't be so
sure. My grounds aren't mere sentimentality, nor are they based
on human reason, fallible as it is. For example, we reason that
if God is just, we may fashion him after our model of justice—a
replica of Oliver Wendell Holmes or Lord Wiggery, elevated of
course to a position as a *Supremely* Supreme Court justice. But
in our very reasonableness, we forget that God isn't an ap-

pointee of some democratic or parliamentary process. He is Absolute and Sovereign, King of Kings and Lord of Lords. From his judgments there is no appeal. In this awareness, therefore, I seek to understand the tenets of Scripture.

From Romans 1 and 2, we obtain Paul's description of natural man, divided into three classifications. The first represents those who, "although they knew God, . . . neither glorified him as God nor gave thanks to him" (Romans 1:21). These are willful rejecters; in consequence of their exercise of will, "God gave them over in the sinful desires of their hearts . . . to shameful lust . . . to a depraved mind" (Romans 1:24, 26, 28). "There are only two kinds of people in the end," wrote C. S. Lewis in *The Great Divorce*, "those who say to God, 'Thy will be done,' and those to whom God says, in the end, '*Thy* will be done.' All that are in Hell, choose it."

The next two classes in Paul's description are those who acknowledge God and who claim to live by his revealed law—either the general moral law or the special revelation of the Law of Moses. This latter group is the Jews, and upon them falls harsh condemnation for their self-righteousness. Although failing to keep the Law, the Jew supposes himself favored by possessing the Law. Instead, says Paul, he is subject to the sternest penalty of that Law, namely death.

But of the middle group Paul has this word:

> (Indeed, when Gentiles, who do not have the law, do by nature things required by the law, they are a law for themselves, even though they do not have the law, since they show that the requirements of the law are written on their hearts, their consciences also bearing witness, and their thoughts now accusing, now even defending them.) This will take place on the day when God will judge men's secrets through Jesus Christ, as my gospel declares (Romans 2:14-16).

This, of course, is the passage most in dispute. It deserves to be read in its full context, which means in relationship to everything else the writer of this closely reasoned essay says about the all-pervasiveness of sin and the character of God in providing justification. Seen in that context, this passage expands to greater breadth than some evangelicals would allow.

First, it's important for us to differentiate the theoretical from the real. Theoretically, Paul avers, it's possible for Gentiles—heathens ignorant of the gospel—to follow perfectly the moral law, the light of nature, the light that lightens every man. In reality, as Paul shows, no one does so. Instead, the natural man understands through the witness of his conscience how far short he falls of the highest standards he knows. He comes under "the requirements of the law" written on his heart. Here Paul declares no theory but the reality of divine justice. For "on the day when God will judge men's secrets through Christ Jesus," some heathen will be able to call their consciences to witness on their behalf.

Not because they have lived sinless lives; on the contrary, they too will have missed the mark that moral law sets for every man. But these will be devout pagans who, in the presence of sin, have been ashamed, have cried out in spiritual anguish, and confessed to whatever representation of the Holy they acknowledge. The difference between them and the rest of the masses outside of faith in Christ is their awareness of evil, their sensitivity to the sting of conscience, and their desire for repentance. According to Paul, his gospel declares them justified "through Jesus Christ."

But how can these who have never heard of Jesus Christ be redeemed through Christ? The mystery of creation is our parallel. Scripture plainly teaches that nothing was made apart from the Creating Word. All that is bears the stamp of his being, whether consciously or not. Whatever life exists originates in him, including that life yet to be produced in some godless laboratory. So too with the new life of redemption. There is no redemption apart from the Redeeming Lord. All who hope for redemption find that hope in him—the devout yet ignorant aborigine as well as the saint—or else there is no redemption for anyone.

The Church of Scotland's Declaratory Act of 1879 supports this view, affirming in Section Four that

> while none are saved except through the mediation
> of Christ . . . it is not required to be held that . . .
> God may not extend his grace to any who are without
> the pale of ordinary means, as it may seem good in
> his sight.

Certainly we dare not exceed God in mercy. The whole question of election, "God's selective purpose" (Romans 9:11, NEB), must be answered by those who can. But neither may we presume to exceed God in judgment, righteousness, or holiness. Thomas Howard reminds us that, like Uzzah who attempted to right the toppling Ark of the Covenant, we can be too scrupulous about protecting the glory of God; like the Pharisees, we can exclude those whose manner of seeking after God distresses us.

There's a temperament that reacts against any deviation from the expected with suspicion and alarm. Perhaps while reading this view of broader redemption, some will take offense and say, "Even if he's right—which he isn't—we can't accept this interpretation because of what it would do to world missions. If you decide that ignorant pagans are saved anyway, first you lose the interest of missionaries. Who wants to go to the jungle and live in a mud hut to tell the heathen something they don't need to hear? Then, the supporters will stop contributing . . ." Have I constructed a straw man? I wish it were so!

Reasoning like this exposes the meanest quality of the evangelical mind—its smugness. On a fund-raising telethon over New York City's Channel 9, a mission leader exhorted his audience to pick up the phone and make a pledge. "Why give to world mission? One reason is you'll like yourself a lot more. You'll look yourself in the mirror and say, 'There's an unselfish person.'"

Smugness is the stench of complacency. It settles for the lowest common denominator in human relationships: our pride, our misplaced sense of personal superiority. We like to think that we have a corner on God's grace because we've satisfied his program for redemption. From spiritual smugness we readily misconstrue our mission to be one of personal gratification while we enculturate or democratize or even civilize the world. But what should be the advantage to a Christian believer? Leonard Hodgson says, "Not the selfish joy of feeling superior to the rest of mankind but the unselfish joy of giving his life in communion with his Master on behalf of all mankind who, equally with himself, are objects of God's love and will to save."

Our only mission is to obey Jesus Christ, who said, "Go and make disciples of all nations" (Matthew 28:19). This should be compelling reason enough. The Great Commission doesn't call us to win souls, to tally numbers of converts, but to *make disciples*. The essence of discipleship is in following the example of the teacher. In the case of Jesus of Nazareth, his disciples are called to join him in announcing good news—the gospel—to the poor, release for prisoners, sight for blinded eyes, healing for victims of disintegrated lives. "The urgency of the preaching of the gospel," says James P. Martin, "arises simply out of the fact that it is the good news of the *only* salvation; the gospel justifies its preaching."

Bishop Reginald Heber of Calcutta sounded the challenge:

> Shall we, whose souls are lighted
> With wisdom from on high,
> Shall we to men benighted
> The lamp of life deny?

This is the message: light, liberty, and life! The gospel in all its enlightening and liberating power must be proclaimed to those whom another hymn writer described as "bound in the darksome prisonhouse of sin." Their fetters have been broken; they no longer need to huddle in the posture of slaves. From the twilight of God's mercy they may pass into the blazing dawn of assurance in God's grace. Best of all, because of the Incarnation, the Cross, and the Resurrection, Christian evangelists can declare the conquering of death. The Lord of the cosmos, as the writer to the Hebrews tells us, has come to share our flesh and blood, "so that by his death he might destroy him who holds the power of death—that is, the devil—and free those who all their lives were held in slavery by their fear of death" (Hebrews 2:14-15).

Our message tells of a Mediator, a Hero to do for us what we can never do for ourselves. Scripture allows no suggestion that man may assert his self-sufficiency and still be a recipient of God's grace because grace issues from faith; in turn, faith begins with a recognition of sovereignty outside ourselves. "Anyone who comes to [God]," says Hebrews 11:6, "must believe that he exists and that he rewards those who earnestly seek him." So, salvation is for those who know they need to be saved!

This is the Good News that billions are still waiting to hear. The program for evangelism is straightforward, based on obedience. In the word of the Lord to Ezekiel, God gives two examples of extreme possibilities in his justice: a believer is responsible for his own sin and he is held accountable to warn both the sinner and the righteous to give up their sin (Ezekiel 3:16-21). We're commanded to proclaim the message; in love, we ought to respond. How that message is received, though it will be our concern, isn't our responsibility. Moreover, what God chooses to make of the results of any faithful witness is also beyond our scope.

THE SUPREMACY OF THE REDEEMER

In proclaiming the message of light, liberty, and life, the evangel must not slight the One in whose name he brings the Good News. "Salvation is found in no one else," said Peter to the council at Jerusalem, "for there is no other name under heaven given to men by which we must be saved" (Acts 4:12). Peter's insight into the power of the Name derives, first, from his personal experience of needing a Savior. "Go away from me, Lord; I am a sinful man!" Peter had exclaimed at his initial meeting with Jesus of Nazareth (Luke 5:8). Some three years later, Peter had lost his courage and turned his back on Jesus. But now, barely two months after the night of his denial, Peter knew whereof he spoke.

The name of the Lord had been known from the sons of Adam, both in cursing and in blessing. But at Babel, mankind attempted to make a name for himself, thereby throwing the Lord's name into abuse. From Babel on, every human accomplishment had been wrongly attributed to Man, so much so that by the time of Israel's bondage in Egypt, Moses had to inquire of God his name. The answer he received, "I am who I am" (Exodus 3:14), spells out qualities of being and eternality inherent in the Most High God. His name became known as Yahweh, Jehovah, the God of Abraham, Isaac, and Jacob. Isaiah 47:4 declares,

> Our Redeemer—the LORD Almighty is his name—
>   is the Holy One of Israel.

Interestingly, except as a figure of speech, God doesn't claim the name of Father.

Yet none of these names was chosen for the Incarnate Lord, whose pre-Incarnation name is the Word. He was to be Emmanuel, God-with-Us, the Prince of Peace, the Branch, Shiloh, Son of David, Son of Man, Son of God. His particular human name, Yeshua or Jesus, means Savior. But his followers knew him as Messiah or Christ, God's anointed Messenger. In time, they also began to call him Lord, not merely a courtesy similar to "Sir," nor the honorific due a nobleman. They saw him to be both Lord and Christ in testimony of his cosmic authority over nature's elements, over atomic particles, over space and time, over disease and demons, and climactically over death. The earliest Christian creed—perhaps also a password among persecuted believers—may have been the three simple words *Kyrios Iesous Christos*, "Jesus Christ is Lord."

Thus Peter's assertion of "no other name" isn't narrowly restricted to the name of Jesus in the sense that certain precise phonemes combine to spell, in English, *J-e-s-u-s*. Peter offers no cabalistic incantation of the name itself. Peter's purpose is to enlarge upon his audience's awareness of the man known as Jesus of Nazareth. But, then, that name is no stranger to this audience! The very politicians present—Annas the High Priest, Caiaphas, Jonathan, Alexander, and the rest—had been present at Jesus' trial and had called for his crucifixion not more than sixty days before. Thereafter these same officials had been thrown into a frenzy by rumors of his body's disappearance from the tomb. While they didn't believe in the purported resurrection, they did know three things: the body was gone; the calumnies against the Roman guard—that they'd been asleep on duty when the body was stolen—were false because these officials themselves had paid the bribes to establish the cover-up; and lastly a strange fervor possessed the followers of Jesus in telling their resurrection story.

What, then, is Peter's objective? To declare not only the name of Jesus but the source of power inherent in that name. The name *Jesus* designates only one characteristic of the Incarnate Word: he is Savior and Redeemer. But more than this: he is *Lord*, he is the *Lord* Jesus, he is the *Lord* Jesus Christ. It is his power as Lord of the universe, not his anglicized name, that saves.

But make no mistake. It *is* Jesus who is Lord. Divine authority has been invested solely in him. Therefore from him must we seek our salvation and to him alone attribute redeeming grace in our lives. It is Jesus in whom God the Father is well pleased; Jesus, as the hymn quoted in Philippians 2:5-11 tells us, who has received the Father's highest exaltation in being given "the name that is above every name."

Yet universal recognition and obeisance have been withheld, awaiting his cosmic coronation. Every sentient being "in heaven and on earth and under the earth" will assemble, brought together for the purpose of acclaiming One Lord. The moment has no equal. Who will it be? Pretenders from every sphere, every galaxy as well as from Satan's stronghold, will be present with their troops to seize the honor and authority. Then thundering through space comes one final pronouncement: Jesus Christ is Lord!

What follows this cosmic disclosure fulfills Isaiah's prophecy,

"By myself I have sworn,
  my mouth has uttered in all integrity
  a word that will not be revoked:
Before me every knee will bow;
  by me every tongue will swear."

(Isaiah 45:23)

The act of genuflecting—the knee bent in homage—acknowledges Jesus' right to authority. A spoken confession completes the submission of every rival power to his Lordship. All this holy drama has but one purpose: to glorify the Father, for whom one consummating act remains.

But before turning to that conclusion, a question needs to be considered. Is the recognition that Jesus is Lord offered willingly or grudgingly? If willingly, does it, at the last, satisfy God's requirement, spoken by Jesus in John 5:23, "that all may honor the Son just as they honor the Father"? And if unwillingly, does its reluctance invalidate the gesture, confirming instead the rebellious nature typified by John Milton's Satan when he says, "Better to reign in Hell than serve in Heaven"? Does anyone but God know?

Now from an eschatological metaphor of coronation, we shift to another apocalyptic image, the Son's claim to his Father's legacy. Where rights of primogeniture are a social norm, transfer of an estate may come to the firstborn whenever his father wishes. But schemes to defraud the legitimate heir are also common. Literature is full of stories about contested estates and impostors who rob the rightful heir. Paul takes this legal theme and uses it metaphorically throughout his letters, especially in Romans.

As God's Son, the Lord Jesus Christ is rightful heir to his Father's possessions; as adopted children by faith, we are also privileged to share that inheritance: "Now if we are children, then we are heirs—heirs of God and coheirs with Christ" (Romans 8:17). But the Impostor, the Great Deceiver, has wrenched away God's prize possession, the universe created for and by his Son. As a result, our universe, or that part known to us, has been imprisoned by sin, cut off from the rest of the cosmos, made the victim of frustration (Romans 8:20). We are "the bent World," in Gerard Manley Hopkins's phrase. Our relationship to the Center has been so distorted and our reason so twisted, any effort to free ourselves ends in further bondage. Like the old drunken vagrant of Edwin Arlington Robinson's poem, "Mr. Flood's Party," we resign ourselves to disintegration and loneliness, "knowing that most things break." Indeed, our planet itself is in physical distress groaning, Paul says, "as in the pains of childbirth" (Romans 8:22).

In this abysmal condition we have continued so long that pessimism and despair seem rational. But not so, Paul declares, for always there was hope "that the creation itself will be liberated from its bondage to decay and brought into the glorious freedom of the children of God" (Romans 8:21). This is God's special gift to his Son, the Father's legacy, giving back to him as Lord what is his by right—an unshackled universe! This glorious prospect, Paul assures us, has always been part of God's secret:

> And he made know to us the mystery of his will according to his good pleasure, which he purposed in Christ, to be put into effect when the times will have reached their fulfillment—to bring all things in heaven and on earth together under one head, even Christ (Ephesians 1:9-10).

When Jesus is enthroned as Lord, the cosmic effect of his New Life, in body as well as in spirit, will manifest itself in a redeemed universe—not merely restored but renewed! From a corruptible state of entropy and decay, our bodies and our universe, under the galvanic energy of the Resurrection, will take on incorruptible form—as Paul instructs the Philippians— "like that of his own resplendent body, by the very power which enables him to make all things subject to himself" (Philippians 3:21).

Then the celebration begins! In the New Jerusalem, we shall be summoned to fulfill Adam's destiny and present our final offering to our Lord, the ultimate work of art—that is, ourselves: formed by the will of the Father, redeemed of our misshapen choices by the Word-Made-Flesh, and burnished to brilliance by the illumining Spirit. We'll participate in furbishing the City of God, for when the apostle John reveals that "the glory and honor of the nations will be brought into it" (Revelation 21:26), he points beyond all corruptible elements of material wealth, the treasures of earth to be left behind. Instead, isn't he describing the splendor of redeemed humanity, fulfilling at last our long-frustrated urge to produce something worthy of praise to God? For then our cultural dross will have been burned away, leaving us free to join in lasting expressions of praise, to sing celestial hymns throughout eternity.

There we'll find the unveiling of a Beauty too rapturous now to contemplate. No longer merely in the eye of the beholder, we shall see and know Beauty himself. The glory of God, radiant like some priceless jewel, will be our light, and we shall see him face to face. His invitation will be to refresh ourselves with thirst-quenching water and to pick a pomegranate from the Tree of Life.

Then the promise that forever marks the passing of the old order: God will wipe away every tear, for there shall be no more death. *No more death?* Except, perhaps, for those who choose it. Except for those who refuse to yield, even when confronted by incontrovertible evidence that Jesus Christ is Lord, those who cannot bring themselves to submit to his Lordship. For them, the Scriptures declare, God will reserve "the second death" in "the fiery lake of burning sulfur" (Revelation 21:8). Not because God wills it so, but because to the very end God prefers to allow his creature the freedom to love, the freedom to worship, the freedom to obey. With this freedom must also go its contrary options—to despise, to blaspheme, to rebel. So the weight of Scripture affirms God's refusal to admit to his Welcome-Home Party anyone who does not wish to be there. The "cowardly, the unbelieving, the vile, the murderers, the sexually immoral, those who practice magic arts, the idolaters and all liars" (Revelation 21:8) are condemned not for their sins— for who among the blessed in Heaven has not also committed these same sins? They are condemned for choosing to remain rebellious against the One who offers to deliver them from their sins. They reject God's *apokatastasis*, preferring to remain addicted to their cowardice and faithlessness and abomination, bound down by murder, lust, witchcraft, and idolatry, enslaved by the Father of Lies. With Satan they are more at home. Thus again, as Lewis said, "All that are in Hell, choose it."

And will some choose it? God leaves that possibility ajar, while remaining unwilling that any should perish. Nonetheless, Jesus Christ declares that on the day of Final Judgment, he himself will say to some, "Depart from me, you who are cursed, into the eternal fire prepared for the devil and his angels" (Matthew 25:41). We have no alternative, therefore, but to accept the probability—yes, the tragic certainty—that some rebels will go—sullen and cursing, or careless and laughing—their way into eternal damnation.

If so, how then can Heaven be joyous, if we know of even one soul willingly given over to perdition? How can Heaven not be full of remorse and regret if families find missing from the circle of loved ones this or that member? How, indeed!

Sentimentally, we sing and talk about family reunions in heaven: "Tell Mother I'll be there in answer to her prayer." But the Scriptures are clear in stating that heaven knows no continuation of earthbound human relations. Jesus rebuked the Sadducees with these words: "You are in error because you do not know the Scriptures or the power of God. At the resurrection people will neither marry nor be given in marriage; they will be like the angels in heaven" (Matthew 22:29-30). At this ultimate, celestial Family Reunion, it is as sons and daughters of God the Father that we assemble. The realization of the Presence of God will make us oblivious to every other relationship we have ever known. Those who have brought us a foretaste of Heaven itself will now be absorbed in the experience of immediate heavenly reality and sublimity; those whose earthly lives have hinted at the horrors of Hell will likewise be as distant from us as is the abyss at the bottom of the great gulf. Why? Because God himself will be with his people, and "he will wipe every tear from their eyes" (Revelation 21:4).

All the old grievances—our rivalries and jealousies separating brother from brother, those political differences making opponents of neighbors, that stupid striving after evanescent and meaningless achievement—all will be forgotten, *wiped away*. All physical deformity, every emotional scar, each stabbing ache of conscience, all pain and suffering, all mourning and weeping, will be gone, eradicated, *wiped away*. My father, E. A. Lockerbie, used to say, "Who wouldn't want to have just one tear to shed when God himself will wipe it away?" Finally, climactically, the last enemy will also submit: "There will be no more death" (Revelation 21:4). Obliterated, *wiped away*.

No more death. The three most glorious words in human experience, provided that they are accompanied by the eternal prospect of life equally free from mourning, crying, and pain. These promises go hand in hand. But what about freedom from heavenly boredom, suffocating sanctimony, and the glissandi of angelic harps for aeons of bliss?

I'm not a terribly comfortable wedding guest. Most weddings bore me; some wedding receptions, too. But I well remember one wedding at which I was neither uncomfortable nor bored, one marriage supper at which I was wholly animated, a honeymoon during which I entertained no regrets. My own— our own—Lory's and mine! It still goes on, these many years later, getting better and better with time.

The New Testament vividly presents its imagery of Bridegroom and Bride, wedding solemnities and marriage feast. And following this celebration, one event remains: a heavenly honeymoon, a marriage literally made in Heaven, that grows better and better for all eternity, *in saecula saeculorum*, world without end, Amen.

Scripture Index

Subject Index

Abraham, 88-89
Accommodation
  and the gospel, 158
  and heresy, 162
  principle of, 156
  without compromise, 162-69
Adam, 88
Advertising, 27-28, 37-38, 56,
  147-49
Antichrists, 147-49
Armageddon, 40
Atheism, 76

Baillie, D. M., 130-31
Baillie, John, 173
Baldwin, James, 106
Barrett, William, 80-81
Beauty, 23
Behaviorism, 42-49
Bellah, Robert N., 105
Berkouwer, G. C., 172
Blackburn, H. J., 52
Blaikie, Robert J., 153
Blanshard, Brand, 43-44
Boredom, 36
Browne, Edward H., 161
Brunner, Emil, 31

Camus, Albert, 59-60, 144
Carelessness, 67
Center, the
  and cosmology, 122
  Incarnation and, 125, 137-42
  loss of the, 117
  and worship, 121
Charlatanism, 149

Christianity
  and culture, 25, 163
  in Japan, 162-65
  and secularism, 26-27
Christmas, 156
Civil religion, 105-6, 109, 111
Complacency, 179
Conceptualists, 79
Cosmology, purpose of, 116
Creation, 22-23
Crime, 40
Culture. *See also* Society
  and Christianity, 25, 163
  cross, 18, 163
  debasement of, 24-32
  Eastern, 17
  ersatz, 26
  Japanese, 163
  preservation of, 19-24
  reverence toward, 22
  sameness, 16-17
  secular, 150
  Toynbee on, 24
  unified world, 22
  Western, 17, 21, 24, 102

Death
  conquering of, 180
  reminder of, 27-30
  second, 186
Debauchery, 65
Delphi, 118-21
Depravity, 152
Dignity, 51
Doomsday, 150
Dostoevski, 74

191